"Lone on the land, and homeless on the water,
  Pass I in patience till the work be done.

Yet not in solitude, if Christ anear me
  Waketh Him workers for the great employ.
O not in solitude, if souls that hear me
  Catch from my joyaunce the surprise of joy!"

F. W. Myers.

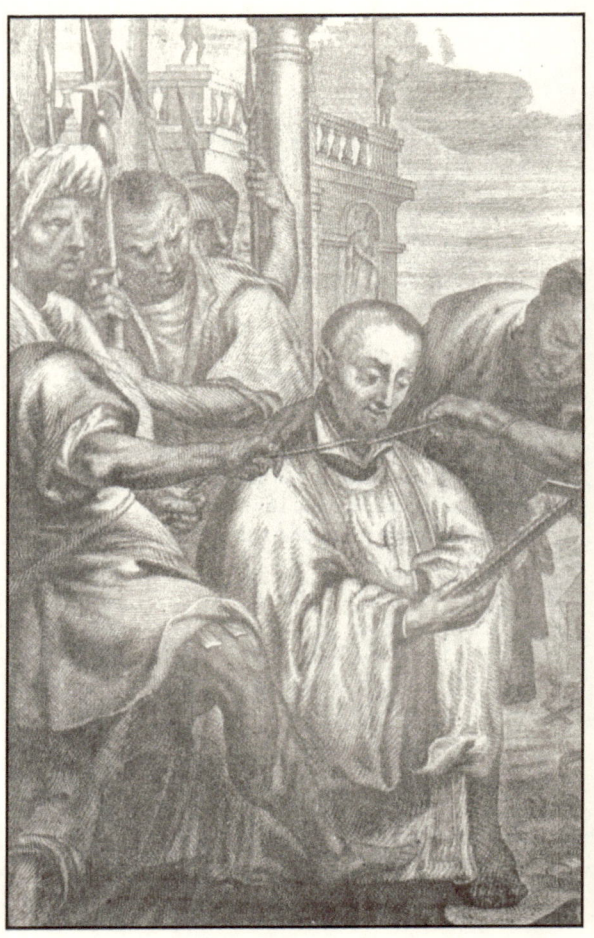

LIFE
OF THE VENERABLE
GONÇALO DA SILVEIRA

OF THE SOCIETY OF JESUS

Pioneer Missionary and Proto-Martyr of Southern Africa

FROM ORIGNAL SOURCES

BY

HUBERT CHADWICK S.J.

Dolorosa Press
Camillus, New York
2018

Nihil Obstat:
> F. THOS. BERGH, O.S.B.
> *Censor Deputatus.*

Imprimatur:
> ✠ PETRUS Epus. Southwarc.

Southwarci, die 27ᵃ Maii 1910.

ISBN: 978-0-9913112-9-3

The Cover is taken from the Rhodesian Tapestry, which is a series of embroidered panels that depict various elements of Rhodesian (Zimbabwean) history. The original plans for the tapestry date back to 1946, when Lady Kate Tait, wife of the then (ex-) Governor of Southern Rhodesia, Sir Campbell Tait, suggested that an embroidery should be made that depicted the "cardinal events in Rhodesian history on the lines of the Bayeux Tapestry" (Ransford 1971:4).

Upper: Scenes from the life and missionary travels of Fr. da Silveira; dugout canoes used for river transport and on right, baptism of a convert. *Lower*: Fr. da Silveira's church.

To order additional copies, please contact:

Dolorosa Press
www.dolorosapress.com

Email: avemaria@dolorosapress.com

TABLE OF CONTENTS

CHAPTER I.
In the Beginning — 1

CHAPTER II.
The Ripening of the Seed — 17

CHAPTER III.
Labours in India — 35

CHAPTER IV.
An African Harvest — 49

CHAPTER V.
At the Court of the "Golden Emperor" — 71

CHAPTER VI.
The Sacrifice — 89

CHAPTER VII.
Flotsam — 102

Appendix — 111

Ve do Benomotapa o grande imperio
De selvatica gente negra e nua,
Onde Gonçalo morte, e vituperio
Padecera pela fé santa sua.
                    Camoens (Lusiadas x. 93).

PREFACE

In the following pages an attempt is made to unearth from beneath the dust of forgotten records the life-story of a holy, austere priest, who, from the remote cloisters of Coimbra, went forth to take his place in history as the pioneer of Christ's Gospel and of European discovery in the heart of Southern Africa. Nursed in the cradle of the Society of Jesus, living amongst men who had learnt from the very lips of their saintly founder the principles of sanctity and self-sacrifice, he was appointed, by the order of St. Ignatius himself, the first regularly constituted successor of St. Francis Xavier as Provincial of the Indies. He was but thirty years old at the time of his appointment: and at the close of his Provincialate, at an age when the Jesuit of to-day is still awaiting the imposition of hands, he crossed the frontiers of civilization to erect the Standard of Christ in a land of shadow and of mystery. He was not, indeed, the very first European to set foot in the country now known by the name of Rhodesia. On his arrival at the kraal of the Makaranga chief, Fr. da Silveira found more than one Portuguese who, for purposes of trade and perhaps for other reasons, had established themselves in the present Lomagundi district. But if he was not actually the first European to live in Rhodesia, he was the first Christian to die there. And his death was that of a martyr, who voluntarily gave up his life for the sake of the generations that were to come after him. He died, that his message of love might live. And if his enterprize resulted in present failure, yet the fruits of his mission may be seen in the centuries that followed his death, and in the progress which Christianity has made, and is still making, in the land of his adoption. The Catholic Church and Christianity owe much indeed to that death by the waters of the Musengezi. The "Proto-martyr" of South Africa may well be an object of legitimate pride to all, and especially to the countrymen of his birth and of his death. For the heroism and enthusiasm of Fr. da Silveira in the cause of Christ's Kingdom makes appeal, not to the Catholic alone, but to the missionary of every creed, and indeed to every man or woman who has learnt the lesson of self-sacrifice, and can appreciate the nobility of altruism in its highest manifestation. As we write, the cause of Fr. da Silveira is being vigorously prosecuted in Rome, with a view to his speedy Beatification. And it is not unworthy of notice that, on less technical grounds, a movement has already been initiated in Rhodesia towards the erection of a monument at Bulawayo, which may serve to perpetuate the memory of one of South Africa's greatest and noblest pioneers.

The praises of da Silveira have long ago been sung by Portugal's most favoured poet. But Portugal is not the only nation which has reason to honour the memory of this Jesuit missionary. On purely secular grounds, the expedition of Fr. da Silveira to Southern Rhodesia must be recognized as the first of a long series of events which has resulted in the present political and social condition of South Africa. Hence it is that the mission to the Monomotapa of 1560—1 belongs not merely to Church history, but to the history of civilization and of colonial expansion. And if this be so, it is surely needless to offer any apology for a sketch, however brief and inadequate, of the life-work of one whose memory for too long a time has been sunk in obscurity.

Fr. da Silveira was not an Englishman: and it is possible that the personality of the man may not appeal, in every respect, to the temperament of another race. As a matter of fact, his personal character is little known to us. The details of his life are gathered from a class of seventeenth century writers, who were mostly content with a record of sanctity rather than of life. As the Bollandist, Fr. Delehaye, has somewhere strongly expressed it: "You ask for a portrait, and you receive a programme." Hagiography, however, is neither synonymous with, nor is it complete without, biography. In the case of Fr. da Silveira, indeed, we are not quite left to our own imagination in our quest of character. From the few letters which have escaped destruction, we may partially reconstruct the picture of a strong-willed, devoted, and austere Religious, going silently about his work, esteeming duty above all else, eager and enthusiastic beyond the very limits of discretion, and recognizing fully and humbly the defects of his own character. This, of course, is but one aspect of the truth. But even in the man as we here find him, there are many qualities which must appeal to every one, no matter what his race or creed. Steadfastness, enthusiasm, self-sacrifice, even unto death, these are characteristics of the man which transcend all limits of time or place. Of the saintliness of his life there can be no question. It has been said of him that, "had he not the glory of a martyr, he would deserve the title of a Confessor of the Faith." It is hoped that the Catholic Church will soon confirm by her decree his claim to the glory of a martyr, in its fullest though more technical sense. But that he was a "martyr of charity," no one has, or can have, any reason to doubt. That this little book may tend in some small measure to spread the fame and to promote the Cause of such a man, is the wish and intention of its author.

May 1st, 1910.

NOTE

The employment in the following pages of the term "martyr" is not, of course, intended to anticipate in any degree the technical decision of the Sacred Congregation, before which, it is hoped, the cause of this Servant of God is shortly to be introduced. The term is used merely in its popular and more extended sense.

I.

In the Beginning.

Whilst in the years 1878-9 the limits of the territory to be assigned to the Jesuits in South Africa were being considered at Rome, numerous reasons were urged why the region lying between the Limpopo and the Zambesi rivers should be included in their sphere of work. And amongst other more material motives, it was not forgotten that this country was especially dear to the Society, as being the scene of the labours and martyrdom of one of its early members. In this land the seed of truth had been planted three centuries ago, and more. By God's most holy Providence, the seed had died: the ground was barren, even though watered with the very life-blood of its first Christian martyr. It is the life and death of that heroic soul, the first Apostle of Rhodesia, which in these pages we propose to relate. A holy, simple story it needs must be, if it is to reflect in any degree the greatness and simplicity of him whose only life-long aim it was to dwell beneath the shadow of the Cross. But let us see it for ourselves.

It was almost under the shadow of the royal castle at Almeirim, a little place some forty miles from Lisbon, that Fr. Gonçalo da Silveira was born, on the 23rd of February, 1526. Thither the King and Court had gone, using the castle as a royal hunting-lodge: and Dom Luis da Silveira, First Count of Sortelha, and a notable officer in the household of Joaõ III., had presumably accompanied his master. The wife of Dom Luis was also of noble family—Dona Brites (or Beatrice) Coutinho, the daughter of Dom Fernando Coutinho, Marshal of the Kingdom. They had already been married for many years: Gonçalo in fact was the Benjamin of the family, the tenth and last child. The Lady Beatrice died in giving him birth, and her husband soon followed her to the little vault where slept in peace the ancestors of his house. But Gonçalo was not unprovided for. His married sister, Dona Philippa de Vilhena, was only too pleased to welcome the little boy at her country home. So Gonçalo travelled north to the seat of his brother-in-law, the Marquis of Tavora, who was the 'overlord' of the district of Mogadouro. Until he went to school, Mogadouro was henceforth his adopted home. His brother, Alvaro, little older than himself, shared the kind home of Dona Philippa. Here they lived together, playmates in the same nursery, under the loving but vigilant eyes of their foster parents. The youth of Dom Gonçalo was not marked, we may suppose, by any very exceptional demonstrations of prodigious piety: though there are not lacking biographers who tell us that the future martyr, some three days even before his birth, was heard to fill his mother's womb with sounds of piteous wailing, "in anticipation, perhaps," suggests Fr. Alegambe,[1] "of his future life-long sorrow for the sins of man." However that may be, we may feel less difficulty in reading of some other characteristics attributed to him. He seems to have always felt the keenest sympathy with the sorrows and troubles of the poor. If he had no alms himself to give, he would often bring back home with him his beggar-friend, and beg in person from his family the needed succour. Especially did he love the little boys of his own age. He would visit them in their homes when they were ill, and bring them presents of food and clothing, bestowing on them the toys which were never of much interest to himself. His sister took great pains in his spiritual training, and he early learnt the value of prayer and pious reading. An interesting anecdote is preserved of this young life which displays his principles

[1] *Mortes Illustres* etc. (Rome, 1657.) Part I. p. 22.

in action. His brother Dom Alvaro and himself had been caught in some harmless escapade; and the matter had been reported to the Marquis. Both were summoned before him and were questioned as to whether they had really done the deed alleged. Alvaro stoutly denied all implication, but Gonçalo admitted the charge. Which of them was speaking the truth? The Marquis resorted to stratagem, and with an angry scowl he turned to Gonçalo, "Wasn't it enough for you to have done wrong," he exclaimed, "but that you must confess it so impudently and without a blush?" "I am indeed ashamed, sir," answered Gonçalo, "and I am sorry for it. But I should have been much more sorry and ashamed, had I tried to save myself from punishment by a lie." The Marquis (it is reported) had no further doubts.[1]

Gonçalo was initiated at home into the mysteries of the alphabet. But the time came when it was necessary to send him to school, to steep himself in the intricacies of Latin and the "Humanities." The Franciscan Monastery of Santa Margarida was finally chosen; and as it was some distance away, beyond the Douro, he was to take up his residence there as a boarder. Gonçalo learnt

[1] Cf. Nicolau Godinho, S.J. *Vita P. Gonzali Sylveria* (Cologne, 1616), p. 9.

to love the Franciscans and their ways. He did more than that: he learnt to imitate them. The Friars used to say in joke that he was quite a Religious except for his clothes. He showed himself very eager and quick in his studies, often sitting up part of the night over his books. Sometimes his valet would grow so weary of waiting to attend him to bed that he would fall asleep outside the door. But he was in no danger of being roughly awakened by his little master. Gonçalo would rise softly to put out the light, and then, without undressing, spend the rest of the night as best he could, in his chair. There were however, many things to be learnt in that monastery besides the cultivation of the intellect. Gonçalo supplemented his reading of numerous Saints' Lives by the living example of simplicity and penance and humility around him. Likely enough the seeds of his vocation were sown in those gentle surroundings. But he was soon to quit the cool, quiet shadows of the Franciscan cloister, for the stir and bustle of a University town. In 1542, while he was yet in his seventeenth year, it was decided that he should continue his higher studies at Coimbra. Thither accordingly he went in the spring of that year, and took up residence at the Monastery of Santa Cruz, belonging to the

Canons Regular. He spent about a year at the University, living, we are told, as befitted his rank, but never forgetting the lessons of assiduity and kindness which he had learnt from the Franciscan Friars.

It was only some few years back that King João III. had at last permanently transferred the University of Portugal from Lisbon to Coimbra. That was in 1537; and three years later, at his earnest request, two members of the newly-instituted Society of Jesus entered his kingdom. They were both destined for the Indian Mission: but it was finally determined that Francis Xavier alone should go, and that Simon Rodriguez should remain behind to establish the Society in Portugal. The former had sailed for Goa in the April of 1541; on the following Epiphany Fr. Simon Rodriguez and two scholastics who had joined him were installed at Lisbon in the fine house and Church of Sant' Antonio Abad. This was the first House of the Society established outside of Rome. A few months later, in June, 1542, the band of Jesuits, now increased to twelve in number, set out at the King's request to start a College at Coimbra. The more worldly inhabitants of that locality were somewhat amused at the sight of these new arrivals. And in truth their appearance and their mode of address were calculated to arouse a certain amount of comment. Only one or two could speak or understand the native tongue. Some were from Paris, some from Rome; and all were easily recognizable as most genuine sons of poverty. The populace at first would call them ugly names, while the more learned sneered. But within a year the position had changed, and many of the noble youths of the highest families had joined the ranks of the new Order. Amongst these was Gonçalo da Silveira. He amongst others had come to realize that poverty is no dishonour, but "a likeness unto God"; and that for all their broken language and promiscuous origin they were united by closer bonds than family or nationality. Fr. Diego Miron was the Rector of the College, and to him Gonçalo applied for admission.[1] Fr. Miron anticipated trouble. He knew that this resolve of the young nobleman would scarcely meet with the approval of his

[1] Fr. Alegambe (*loc. cit.*) has caused some confusion (*e.g.*, ZAMB. MISS. RECORD, vol. i. p. 139) by his statement that Fr. da Silveira remained "for some years" at the monastery of Santa Cruz. The error may be traced to the authority of Orlandini (*Hist. Soc. Jesu*, pt. i. lib. iv. n. 57), who is himself partially correcting Polanco (*Chron. Soc. Jesu*, i. p. 120). Fr. Franco gives June 9, 1543, as the date of his entrance into the Society (v. "*Imagem da virtude em o noviciado ... de Coimbra*" (Coimbra, 1719), vol. iv. p. 5).

relatives, and that Gonçalo would need a large amount of courage in order to withstand their attacks. Consequently, Gonçalo suddenly disappeared from Coimbra. Together with Fr. Miron (and possibly a few other postulants) he had made his way to a small secluded hermitage to the north; and there for a month he busied himself, making, under the Rector's guidance, the Spiritual Exercises of St. Ignatius. What passed in that lonely hermitage we cannot know. Certain it is that on his return to Coimbra a great change had taken place in his life and thoughts. A strange earnestness was remarked in one who even by natural gift was ever serious and thoughtful. The standard of Christ had become for him a cross, all fiery, wet with the "crimson-throbbing" blood of the World-Martyr. It was the idea and the desire of martyrdom that had taken possession of his soul.

Henceforth the life of Gonçalo was a new one. On returning to Coimbra after his month's retreat, he did not go back to his friends the Canons Regular, but to the Jesuit College hard by. Meanwhile, his relatives had sought for him in vain. Hearing that Gonçalo had at length returned as mysteriously as he had gone, his elder brother, Count Diogo, accompanied by some of his kinsmen and friends, presented himself at the door of the College, begging to see his brother. But it was in vain that he used all manner of persuasion and entreaty. Gonçalo was not to be dissuaded from his holy enterprize, by threat or by argument. So powerful indeed were his spirited replies that his brother left him, sorrowing even that the call of God was not for him as well.

For some eighteen months, Gonçalo lived as a novice, undergoing the experiences and trials incidental to such a state. With all the ardour of Southern chivalry, he threw himself into the fight against flesh and blood. The idea of martyrdom was ever before his eyes. That was the one ambition of his spiritual life, colouring his every thought and deed. In his little cell the only objects decorating the walls were four wooden crosses, made by his own hands, with no large expenditure of skill. They hung in the centre of each bare wall, perpetual reminders of a past and of an ideal future. The cell itself was scarcely more inviting than the bare walls. There was a bed, indeed, but he seldom slept in it. Usually he preferred the hard floor, taking for pillow a stone or piece of thick wood. There every night before he went to rest he would discipline himself until the blood flowed. And in numerous other ways did he wage

pitiless, cruel war against himself and whatever **remnants there** were of pride and passion. It **is noted by** all his biographers that many of his actions went beyond the limits of the imitable, and were plainly indiscreet. For instance, he appeared one morning amongst the Community with his eyebrows shaved. At another time he feigned madness by his countenance and gait, hoping to be mistaken for an idiot. The Rector and Master of Novices, Fr. Miron, was nevertheless more than satisfied with the capabilities and promise of Gonçalo. Writing to St. Ignatius in Rome, he thus describes him: "We have with us here one of the nobility, Gonçalo da Silveira by name, . . a young man of sound and sober judgment, born to do great things. He has come to realize the truths of eternity, and has been stirred by such thoughts. He seems to have them stamped on his heart. He is strong and robust in body, and needs to be watched and restrained in his excessive austerities. But he is very tractable and responsive when corrected. He possesses remarkable gifts."[1] . . . He was given the charge, both spiritual and temporal, of some African or Indian domestics, who helped the few lay-Brothers in the work of the house. Later in life he was destined to do great work

[1] Alegambe, *op. cit.* p. 23.

for both these peoples. Meanwhile, he took delight in attending most assiduously to those committed to his care; and there was no office, however menial, he would not do for them, visiting them when sick, and making their beds, putting the very food and medicine into their mouths. Bartoli describes most vividly[1] how one day Gonçalo was assisting at the lancing by the doctor of an abscess in the foot of one of his charges, and how, whilst carrying away the matter from the room he experienced a nausea at the sight and smell. To overcome himself he immediately swallowed the object of his imagined fastidiousness.

At the end of his formal Noviceship, on November 1, 1544, he took the usual simple vows of poverty, chastity, and obedience. To these he added three others, out of devotion: 1st, that he would never, either directly or indirectly, seek any relaxation from his vows; 2nd, that he would never take even an alms in return for spiritual services; 3rd, that he would never willingly leave the Society or its manner of life; if he should be dismissed he would try to return; and that in any case he would join no other Order, unless his Superiors should advise him to do so. Ten months

[1] Bartoli, *Degli Uomini e de'Fatti*, &c., iii. p. 194. (Turin, 1847.)

later, on the feast of our Lady's Nativity, September 8, 1545, the sacred dignity of the priesthood was conferred upon him, after little more than two years' experience of religious life.

Thus did he rivet himself as closely as possible to the object of his love. He still remained at Coimbra for some five years more, pursuing his studies with great diligence and success. Nor did his life differ much from the older life of a novice. Only the enthusiastic outbreaks of intemperate piety became less frequent, more controlled. Yet excess was ever a difficulty in his life. Struggle as he would, his southern blood could not but burst its barriers. At all events, it was a fault which arose from largeness, not from littleness of soul; and there is often something very grand and noble, even in his faults. Whilst Gonçalo was at Coimbra, it was judged necessary to build a new College. Fr. Simon Rodriguez, the Provincial, laid the foundation-stone in April, 1547. All the scholastics and lay-Brothers—and there were over a hundred of them—spent such time as they could spare from their other work in assisting the builders. Gonçalo was often to be seen carrying bricks and stones, or driving a mule through the streets of the town, with its load of sand from the river-bed. One day he met his brother, Dom Alvaro, in the street. Dom Alvaro felt ashamed of his beggar brother, and tried to look the other way. But Gonçalo was quite unabashed. Never before had he used his voice and stick so well to urge on his astonished mule. Dom Alvaro's feelings may be imagined as he listened to his brother's shouts and cries dying away in the distance. In truth, Gonçalo was always somewhat unbending towards his kinsmen. At one period he was pestered by the insistence of the ladies of the Court, who wished to see him and hear him preach at the Royal Palace. He soon perceived that not his sermons but he himself was the principal feature of these ceremonies. To escape their attentions, he let himself grow dirty—disgustingly dirty to our modern, northern ideas; and his brother, Count Diogo, evidently was disgusted too. But he could not change Gonçalo's purpose. "I'd sooner have animals crawling over me than be a Count," was his embarrassing reply. On a later occasion he was invited by his sister, Dona Philippa, and her husband to come and visit them at Goes. His answer was pathetic, begging her not to draw him into the world again. Though he was related to her by blood, he reminded her, yet in a far higher, transcendent sense was he related to Christ, by that Blood in which, as a priest, he daily communicated. But Dona Philippa, for reasons unexplained, did not desist from her request. The Rector was finally induced by the Marquis of Tavora to order Gonçalo to comply with the wishes of his family. Yet Gonçalo laid down his conditions, all the same. He and his companion, Melchior Carneiro, were to be given a lodging apart from the rest of the house; they were to have their meals in their own room; and they would treat the slave who attended upon them, not as an inferior, but as an equal in all respects to themselves. His sister was too anxious to have him at all to cavil at the cost. Certainly, the example which he set to all the household was recompense enough, in spite of what she might most pardonably have considered want of manners. But she could make allowances for her enthusiastic brother; she had the great advantage of knowing and understanding him thoroughly—which we have not. Yet there was one thing which even she could never enter into, and that was his ever-constant love of martyrdom. "But I shouldn't like you to be a martyr," she would tell him; "I am frightened by the very idea of such a thing. I shall be quite satisfied to see you a really holy priest." On such occasions Gonçalo would wax eloquent in speaking of the dignity and excellence of the martyr's crown. He had evidently volunteered for service in the "white-robed army." But he could never quite reconcile his sister to the idea. Before he left, she begged him to obtain for her from God the favour that she should bear her husband a little boy as heir to his estate and name. For as yet God had not given them a son. "It will be all right," said Gonçalo. And in less than ten months' time a baby son was added to the nursery. His influence upon his family and relations did not cease at his departure. A younger sister, Dona Leonor Coutinho, fired by the example of her still younger Jesuit brother, though on the very point of marrying, determined to leave all and enter a convent. A similar story is told of one of Gonçalo's nieces, presumably an elder daughter of his sister Philippa.

But to return to his career at Coimbra. In 1548, we hear of his taking charge of the novices; and Fr. Emmanuel Godinho bears testimony to his success in that important office.[1] It was in this same year that Fr. Simon Rodriguez, the Provincial, paid a memorable visit to the rising college. Not long after his arrival, he one day summoned

[1] *Monumenta Historica S.J.: Epist. Mixta*, vol. i. p. 532.

to his presence Fr. Luis de Grana (who had entered the Society in the same year as Gonçalo), and informed him that he was to be the new Rector of Coimbra. He then called Fr. Luis Gonzalez de Camara, who was Rector at the time, and gave him work for a while in the kitchen. Fr. Gonzalez appears to have been well content with his new, though of course, not permanent office. Whilst Fr. Rodriguez was in the house, he had occasion to perform a service of a different kind for Gonçalo. For Gonçalo happened at the time to be very ill: so much so that his very life was in the balance. The Provincial visited him one morning on his way to Mass. "Cheer up, Gonçalo," he said, "I'm going to offer up my Mass for your recovery." Before the Mass was over, Gonçalo suddenly exclaimed, in the presence of Fr. Luis de Grana and three others, who were there, that he was cured. And so it proved to be. For some while after his recovery he was even anxious to change his name to Silvester, in memory of the feast on which this favour was vouchsafed.[1]

[1] Orlandini, *Hist. Soc. Jesu*, part 1, lib. viii. n. 80.

II.

The Ripening of the Seed.

ST. IGNATIUS had long wished to see Fr. Simon Rodriguez once again, and to confer with him in person upon the subject of the organization of his Province. This seemed the more urgent, as certain reports had reached him as to his Provincial's conduct of affairs which caused him some anxiety. Accordingly, in the summer of 1549 he had written to King João, asking leave of absence for Fr. Simon. But the King was not anxious to lose his friend: yet the matter had gone so far that in December, 1549, Fr. Gonçalo received a letter, ordering him to proceed with four companions to Valencia, and there to await his Provincial's arrival. They were afterwards to accompany Fr. Simon to Rome,[1] to help in the re-adjustment of affairs. The party of five, all priests, left Coimbra on the feast of the Epiphany,

---

[1] De Backer (*Bibliothèque des Ecrivains*, &c., Second Series, p. 611) states incorrectly that Fr. Gonçalo actually went to Rome. His notice contains several inaccuracies, which are repeated almost verbatim in Fr. Sommervogel's new edition. (*Bibliothèque de la Compagnie de Jésus*, Brussels, 1896, vol. vii. p. 1731.)

1550, to the sorrow of the Community.[1] After a journey of some few days they arrived in Spain at the town of Ciudad Rodrigo, where they lodged for the night at the hospital. Many of the nobility of the town took the opportunity of making acquaintance with members of this far-famed Society, and of consulting them upon various matters of the soul. It was not till after midnight that the Fathers managed to obtain a little rest. Next morning, complying with the wishes of the townspeople, Fr. Gonçalo preached at the hospital, with great harvest of penitence and confession. That same day they continued their journey eastwards. At Salamanca they were received with great kindness and courtesy by Fr. Miguél de Torres, Rector of the Jesuit College. They were detained for some four or five days at Avila by reason of a heavy snowstorm which rendered the roads almost impassable. Here again Fr. Gonçalo preached, with no less fruit than at Ciudad Rodrigo. But as soon as the snow had melted somewhat, the company trudged on again, travelling for fully ninety miles knee-deep in snow. They had come by this

[1] A detailed account of the journey is given in a letter of Fr. Antonio Brandão, one of the company, to St. Ignatius. (V. *Monumenta Historica S.J.: Epist. Mixtæ*, ii. pp. 373—377.)

road in order to visit on their way the Marchioness de las Navas, the aunt of Francisco Borgia, Duke of Gandia. This good lady received them " as a mother," says Fr. Brandão: and during the two days of their stay she scarcely ever left them, plying Fr. Gonçalo and the others with innumerable questions as to the Society and its mode of life, begging even to be admitted in some fashion as a member. One of her sons, aged thirteen, was eager to accompany Fr. Gonçalo on his departure: but he was considered too young. As the Fathers would not accept of presents, she insisted on sending with them a man, with two mules for their baggage, who should show them the road to Alcala. Here they rested a day, and then hurried on to Guadalajara, hoping to see the young Fr. Francisco Strada: but they did not find him there, to their disappointment. At Valencia they expected to meet Fr. Miron, Gonçalo's old Rector at Coimbra: but here again they had miscalculated. So, without delay, they proceeded to Gandia, where they were most warmly welcomed by the Duke, Francisco Borgia, who had not yet openly thrown off his secular disguise. Here Fr. Gonçalo took his Doctorate of Theology at the University in the beginning of March. As he and Fr. Brandão took their degrees some days before the others, they returned at once together to Valencia, where Fr. Gonçalo gave himself up to preaching, filling full the confessional of his companion. For nearly a month they waited, until Easter was come and gone; yet no news reached them to explain the delay of their Provincial. At length Fr. Gonçalo decided to wait no longer, but to return to Portugal. But a difficulty confronted him. On the one hand he had received orders from Simon Rodriguez, in the event of the failure of the expedition, to bring back all his companions to Portugal. Yet on the other hand he was shown a letter, signed by St. Ignatius himself, which enjoined that two of his companions, Fr. Morera and Fr. Cuvillon, should remain at Gandia. Was he to obey his Provincial or his General? He finally decided to obey his immediate Superior; and ordered all his companions to accompany him. Any difficulties, he thought, could be settled later between St. Ignatius and his Provincial. Meanwhile he would act as he judged best, under what must certainly be considered as exceptional and most trying circumstances. It appears that for a time at least this conduct caused some misunderstanding at Rome[1]—a misunderstanding

[1] *Monumenta Historica S.J : Epist. Mixta*, ii. p. 377, note 2.

which in the Society's early days may easily be imagined, in view of the yet undefined limitations of immediate authority, and of the state of administrative organization in the Portuguese Province.

On the return of the Fathers to Portugal they learnt that the cause of Fr. Simon Rodriguez not having met them at Valencia was the refusal of King Joaõ to let him go. In the absence of Fr. Simon from Lisbon, Fr. Gonçalo assumed charge of the Community of Sant' Antonio. The Community at this time numbered fourteen, yet the work was greater than could be coped with. Fr. Gonçalo was busily engaged in preaching and hearing confessions, and in the irksome routine of a Court chaplain. At this period the Jesuits were very popular at Lisbon, and crowds thronged to the services at Sant' Antonio. Especially did the sermons of the young Fr. Gonçalo attract attention. Great fervour was shown at the Friday evening services, when, after a *fervorino* by one of the Fathers, a public *flagellatio* on the part of the congregation took place. It is said that the Queen, hearing of the great increase of devotion which resulted, expressed a wish to be present at these services.

In the spring of the following year, 1551, Fr. Gonçalo received orders to proceed north to Braga, taking Fr. Gaspar Diaz as companion. No money was given them, so they begged their way: and oftentimes they experienced vividly the meaning of a vow of poverty. It will be remembered that one of the extra vows taken by Fr. Gonçalo after his noviceship was that he would accept not even an alms in return for spiritual services. The rigorous observance of this vow often sent him and his companion supperless to bed. Fr. Diaz indeed was not acting under vow in following the example of his companion. But the great edification caused by this manner of living was ample reward for any amount of self-imposed hardship. Passing through Oporto on their way, they were persuaded by the townspeople to delay there for a day or two. And Fr. Gonçalo, whose fame had already travelled beyond the confines of Lisbon, was constrained to preach both in the cathedral, and in some of the other numerous churches of the town. The people were delighted, and entreated him to remain with them at least during Lent. On Fr. Gonçalo urging the prior claims of obedience, they petitioned the Archbishop of Braga for faculty to retain him. But the Archbishop left the matter entirely in his hands, and Fr. Gonçalo, who had already arrived at Braga, some thirty or forty miles distant, decided that it was his duty to remain where he had been originally sent. The Archbishop offered him a lodging in his own house, but the hospitality was gently declined, and the two Jesuits betook themselves to the common hospital. Here they remained during the season of Lent, wearing themselves out by strenuous labours of every kind. The old Gothic cathedral was packed when on the first day of Lent, Fr. Gonçalo ascended the pulpit. But though he more than satisfied his audience, he did not satisfy himself. On the following Friday he preached again, but at the hospital, before the Archbishop and his chapter. This time he acknowledged that even he himself was not displeased with the result; whilst the letters of some of his hearers describe the sermon in unmeasured terms of praise. Thus in missionary labour the weeks passed away; and by the end of Lent he had almost worn himself out, having grown "decidedly weak and thin,"[1] as the chronicler records.

Meanwhile the people of Oporto had obtained the leave of the Rector of Coimbra that Fr. Gonçalo should stop at their city on his return. Here accordingly he remained from Easter to Pentecost, doing good work,

[1] *Monumenta Historica S.J.; Chron. Soc. Jesu*, ii. p. 361.

especially amongst the rich and the nobility.

The rest of the year was spent at Coimbra, which he did not leave until, in the following year, the royal will summoned him to fresh enterprise at Thomar. This was a little town, some forty miles to the south, the occasional residence of the King and Court. Here Fr. Gonçalo remained for two months, with his companion, Fr. Nogheira, performing the usual duties of a missioner. He gained such a place in the affections of the townsfolk that they begged the King to retain him longer. And Fr. Gonçalo, nothing loth to work for Christ, saw six full months go by before he returned to Coimbra. At Thomar, as on all his missionary journeys, he practised the strictest poverty and self-denial. Everywhere the hospital rather than the palace was his place of abode. He begged his food from day to day, addressing himself usually to those who were too poor to give him anything but the very worst. At Oporto, for instance, he might have been seen at the hour of dinner, going along the narrow streets, his beggar's bowl in hand, asking at the poorer dwellings, in the name of Jesus Christ, for a crust of bread. For the same reason he would never beg immediately after preaching, for fear lest in such case the alms should be given rather to him, for his fine sermon, than for love, to our Blessed Lord. Very rarely did he break his custom of sleeping upon the bare ground. In exceptional circumstances he would requisition a straw mattress from the hospital, without sheets or pillow, and luxuriate among the prickles. At times too he would add a little to his meagre fare of bread and water. But he hesitated to do this, unless he were unusually ill or tired. Often enough he would place himself upon his knees at nightfall in the soft, reddened dusk of the sanctuary, and there would keep his vigil, praying until his companion summoned him for Mass next morning. His was in very truth a noble, fruitful life—fit preparation for a death more noble and more fruitful still.

In works and labours such as these did Fr. Gonçalo spend the early years of his priesthood. Space will not allow us to follow the course of his frequent journeys through the towns and villages of Portugal. After leaving Thomar, we catch glimpses of him at Braga or thereabouts, at Oporto again, and in the country district around Coimbra. In the August of this year, 1553, he was for a short while at Evora, in company with Fr. Jerome Nadal, the Commissary-General. Here he preached with even greater success than hitherto. A nun who had heard him in her convent is reported to have said that she had never seen such tears flow in choir as when Fr. Gonçalo preached to her community. After a short stay at Evora, he proceeded to Lisbon for his profession.

The Society had now been established for over ten years in Portugal, and it seemed suitable to Fr. Nadal that another residence should be acquired to serve as a "Professed House." By negotiation with the King and his brother, the Infante Luis, the Church of San Roque, at Lisbon, was handed over for this purpose: and on September 30, 1553, the Jesuits took formal possession. On the day following (Sunday, October 1st), a number of priests and lay-Brothers pronounced their last vows in the church. Three of these took the four public vows of a "professed" Father; namely, Fr. Gonçalo da Silveira, Fr. Gonçalo Vaz, and Fr. Antonio de Quadros. It was a grand ceremony, in presence of the King and Court, and of many of the noblest families of Lisbon. Fr. Francis Borgia preached on the occasion, reminding his hearers of another King and another Court, into whose perpetual service these soldiers of Christ's company were vowing themselves. After the sermon, the Holy Sacrifice was offered by Fr. Nadal, who also received, in the name of the Society, the solemn vows of those who were kneeling in a semi-circle around him.

The three professed remained in Lisbon, Fr. Gonçalo being appointed the first *Præpositus*, or Superior, of San Roque. It is, perhaps, worthy of remark that at this time the Rector of the other Jesuit house at Lisbon, the College of Sant' Antonio, was Fr. Ignatius de Azevedo, who also, in the future years, was to shed his blood upon the "white road."[1]

The two and a half years of Fr. Gonçalo's superiorship passed quietly away. He set himself at once to work, preaching on Sunday and festival mornings at the Church of San Roque, whilst Fr. Vaz would preach in the evenings. The oratorical talents of both these Fathers, and of Fr. Gonçalo in particular, were considered on all sides to be exceptional. Fr. Francisco Viera mentions in one of his letters that "he (*i.e.*, Fr. Gonçalo) displays great ease, and fluency, and fervour in his preaching, and promises well for the future."[2] And the crowds which thronged to hear him are in themselves ample testimony that the praise of Fr. Viera was

[1] He was martyred at sea, off the island of Las Palmas, one of the Canaries, on July 15, 1570.
[2] *Monumenta Historica S.J.: Litteræ Quadrimestres*, ii. p. 536.

rather stinted than exaggerated. Above all was he noted for his earnestness. It is said that in the course of one of his sermons he struck the pulpit by accident where a long nail was projecting from the wood. Though the blood flowed freely from the wound, the incident was not even noticed by the preacher until the close of the discourse. Those were not the days of short sermons. It was quite customary for him to speak for two or three hours at a time: but his fire and brilliancy held the attention of his auditors. At Thomar, one day in Holy Week, he had held his audience entranced for twelve full hours! So at least we are informed by one or more of his biographers.[1]

By the end of the year the building of the new house for the Professed, adjoining the church, had so far advanced that the Fathers were able to take up residence in it. Fr. Gonçalo had apparently expressed a desire to be released from his office, and to go where he was less known and venerated. But his obedience to the will of his Superiors was perfect. As a Superior himself, he was most kind and considerate, and his corrections were gentle and never bitter. At the same time he was very strict in the matter of

---

[1] Cf. Tanner, S.J. *Soc. Jesu usque ad sang. et vitæ profus. militans.* (Prague, 1675). Part i. p. 163.

exemptions, whether in food or lodging, or in any duty of community life. Plagues, he called such relaxations of rule or discipline. Yet his Community loved him all the more, perhaps, for his strength of character. Certainly, at his departure for India, their distress at losing him was plainly seen. And their love and veneration for his holiness were shared by all who knew him. Stories passed from mouth to mouth of his marvellous gifts of prayer: how he had often been found in his chamber, wrapt in ecstasy, and raised from the floor: how, whilst saying Mass, he would so lose consciousness of his surroundings as to be obliged to ask his server where he had left off. Many of these tales were certainly true, whilst some probably arose from the inventive genius of his fellow-citizens. Fr. Gonçalo had an extraordinary devotion for our Blessed Mother. Hour after hour would he remain kneeling before her statue. When reciting her Rosary, he would genuflect at every *Ave*. And on her feasts he would do little else than repeat again and again this Angelical Salutation, never omitting the genuflection. His imitation of her purity would often lead him two or three times a day to the confessional. And in every way, by his utter poverty, his humility, his penance, his contempt of the world and its shadows, did he endeavour to approach ever nearer to that Mother and her Son.

In the spring of 1555 there was talk of sending Fr. Gonçalo as Provincial to India. Some confusion had arisen there as to the validity of the office of the present Provincial of India, Fr. Melchior Nuñez, and of the Vice-Provincial, Fr. Balthasar Diaz.[1] Fr. Gonçalo was all on fire to commence a missionary life abroad. But circumstances delayed his departure until the following year. Meanwhile he began to enlarge the Church of San Roque, which had become far too narrow for the crowded congregation. For a while, indeed, certain unfavourable reports were current in connection with the Professed House: and the Fathers had fallen, to a certain extent, into ill favour with the inhabitants. This Fr. Gonçalo considered in the light of a good omen, saying that the devil was jealous and angry at their success; and their popularity was soon restored, and even increased. Fr. Gonçalo added to his other duties the practice of preaching on Sunday afternoons at the Church of the College of Sant' Antonio. After his departure this duty devolved upon Fr. Ignatius de Azevedo, who, on recovering from a severe illness at the College, had lately been

[1] *Vide* Polanco, *Chron. Soc. Jesu,* iv. p. 642, et seq.

appointed Minister of the Professed House. At last St. Ignatius, some five or six months before his death, approved the appointment of Fr. Gonçalo as Provincial of India.[1] It was feared by some that his departure from Lisbon would cause great inconvenience, and even injury, to the prosperity of San Roque, and certain intrigues were entered into, which do not reflect much credit upon those concerned. Fr. Gonçalo, however, was in no wise disturbed by these measures. It seems clear that in this, as in some other matters, God had gifted His servant with an insight into the future. Some years ago he had prophesied to his incredulous brother, Dom Alvaro,[2] the defeat of his fleet in a battle against the Turks. And other instances are recorded of this miraculous foreknowledge. It was whilst assisting at the execution of a criminal that God had revealed to him the fact and the manner of his future martyrdom. Having delivered a fervent exhortation to the assembled crowd, he had become absorbed in the consideration of Christ's agony upon

[1] Fr. Gonçalo is even said to have petitioned St. Ignatius to be sent on the Foreign Missions. *Vide* Franco, *Annus Gloriosus* . . . (Vienna, 1720), p. 151.

[2] This brother died in 1559 in the Persian Gulf. Cf. Pinheiro Chagas, *Os Portuguezes na Africa, Asia*, &c. (Lisboa, 1890), vol. vi. pp. 152, 153.

the Cross, and he had prayed with his whole soul that it might be granted him to share in those sufferings even unto death. It was then that our Lord gave him the desire of his heart, promising that he should one day die for His name. Fr. Gonçalo often related this in all simplicity, especially to an intimate friend, Fr. Leo Enriquez. He even mentioned it once in a sermon at Lisbon. Indeed, that was the one subject upon which he would always wax eloquent—the glory of a martyr's crown. Upon hearing of the death of Fr. Antonio Criminale, who was killed by the Badages upon the Fishery Coast in the May or June of 1549, he could scarcely contain himself.[1] Later, as Superior of San Roque, he was saying public Mass one morning, and was in the act of elevating the sacred chalice, when, to the eyes of the congregation, his hands appeared all stained with blood. This was understood by all as a sure sign of his future death for the faith of Christ.

So, when the preparations for his voyage were commenced, Fr. Gonçalo felt sure that he was walking more directly towards the goal of his life's ambition. A fleet of four vessels was to sail for Goa on March 28, 1556, and it was arranged that the company

[1] Coleridge, S.J., *Life and Letters of St. Francis Xavier*. ii. p. 194.

of Jesuits should be divided amongst the ships. In the first ship sailed Fr. Juan Nuñez, who had been lately consecrated Patriarch of Ethiopia. The batch in the second vessel was in the charge of Fr. André de Oviedo, Bishop of Hierapolis and Coadjutor of the Patriarch. Fr. Gonçalo was in the third ship with two other Jesuits, one of them a priest. After taking leave of the King and his Court, the company embarked at Lisbon on March 28th, but as the sea was rough, the vessels did not leave harbour till the following Monday (March 30th). The fleet was separated almost at once, but three of the vessels, after encountering some heavy seas round the Cape, arrived by a curious chance on the very same day at Mozambique. On the day following, July 25th, the ship in which Fr. Gonçalo and his companions were sailing, hove in sight. The Provincial had been true to himself during the voyage, attending on all, cooking the food for his two comrades, delighting in every menial office. He slept with the sailors in the forecastle, wrapped in his heavy mantle, the only protection he would use against the winds and the damp of a long voyage. He had been sick during the first few days after leaving Lisbon; and the rest of the journey had not tended to correct his view of the gloominess and discomforts of a sea-voyage. Writing to Fr. Gonçalo Vaz, who succeeded him as Superior of San Roque, he prefaces his account of the voyage by saying: "As death cannot well be described except by one who has attended a death-bed, so the voyage from Portugal to India can only be related, or even believed, by him who has had that experience."[1] The ships remained some eighteen days at Mozambique, and the Fathers were able to do a great amount of good in the island during their stay. Fr. Gonçalo and two other priests slept on shore, so as to afford more opportunity to the people of going to confession without discomfort. On the day after his arrival, having first visited the grotto dedicated to *Nossa Senhora do baluarte*—"Our Lady of the Ramparts,"—he preached a stirring sermon at the "Misericordia." The clergy of this church had been for some while at loggerheads with the Vicar. By the kind offices of the Jesuits, this scandal was finally removed. After frequent sermons and instructions of all kinds during their stay, the company set sail again on the feast of St. Lawrence, August 10th, and with a fair wind they arrived at Goa on September 6th.

[1] "*Diversi Avisi* dall' Indie di Portogallo ricevuti dall' anno 1551, fino al 1558, &c." fol. 283.

III.

Labours in India.

IT was quite dark when the vessels reached the port. Fr. Gonçalo did not wait for the others; but making his way up to Goa by himself, he sought out the Jesuit College, and begged admittance as a stranger. Fr. Antonio de Quadros, the Provincial, who would have recognized him at once as an old friend, had gone down to the port to welcome the new arrivals. So Fr. Gonçalo was admitted by the porter as a guest, bearing recent news from the mother-country. Having thus satisfied his humility, and perhaps his curiosity as well, Fr. Gonçalo assumed his proper position as Provincial of India. On the very next morning he commenced a course of sermons at the cathedral, which he continued every Sunday until his departure for Bassein towards the beginning of November. There was certainly much for him to do. The state of India at this period may be gathered to some extent from the letters which St. Francis Xavier had written home during the previous ten years. The Portuguese in India had for the most part grown effeminate and immoral. And the condition of the native Christians was rendered difficult and even dangerous by the avarice and the cruelty of these forerunners of European civilization. Nor were the Jesuits altogether independent of the Portuguese officials. At Coulan, for instance, where Fr. Lancilotti was conducting a college of some seventy day-scholars, the revenue granted him by the King of Portugal was being withheld by the local authorities.[1] Thus the work was plenty, whilst the labourers were comparatively few. At this time there were almost a hundred Jesuits in the East, of whom sixty were resident at the College of Goa itself.[2] The rest were scattered far and wide along the coasts and islands, from Bassein to the Moluccas and Japan.

The Viceroy, Dom Francisco Barreto, received Fr. Gonçalo very kindly indeed, and, at the latter's request, was pleased to grant numerous petitions on behalf of several who had found the Provincial a ready spokesman for those in want. Thus were many poor

---

[1] Orlandini, *Hist. Soc. Jesu*, part i. lib. xvi. n. 76.

[2] *Ibid.* part i. lib. xvi. n. 71. The sixty at Goa include Scholastics and novices. By the end of 1557, there were twenty Scholastics, and thirty-five novices. (Cf. *Novi Avisi dell' Indie*, &c., fol. 15.)

relieved of their troubles, and many favours gained for the new Christian converts. It was one of the Provincial's first cares to arrange about the establishment of a formal novitiate in India. This he did by reserving for the use of the novices part of the College of São Paulo. Soon afterwards he left Goa with the Viceroy and Fr. de Oviedo, the Coadjutor-Bishop of Ethiopia, and made his way north to Bassein, distant from Goa some 200 miles. As he travelled rather faster than the Viceroy and his suite, he was able to stay a week at Chaul on his way. Here he took up his abode at the usual "hospital," in spite of the entreaties of the Dominicans that he should accept of their fare and lodging. At dinner-time he followed his old custom of going through the streets, begging for bread and water. As this was the first time that a Jesuit had so acted in those parts, he caused some surprise, and was followed back to the hospital by a crowd of all sorts, who insisted upon hearing him preach. The people of Chaul were anxious that he should establish in their town a House of the Society: and they offered the Provincial the Church of São Sebastião, promising to build a residence if he would consent. But Fr. Gonçalo put off the matter, being unwilling to act without the advice of his consultors.

The inhabitants of Thana, a little place twelve miles to the south of Bassein, were prepared to welcome Fr. Gonçalo with torches and procession, as he passed through their town. But he arrived unexpectedly on November 25th, and proceeded to Bassein that same evening. The native Christians, however, were not to be disappointed of their expected rejoicings. After the sermon which he preached to them in the morning, they produced their musical instruments, and struck up a tune in his honour. "Though the music itself was not quite good," he writes somewhat humorously, "yet their energy and good-will was great."[1]

On December 8th,[2] he visited Thana again for a few days, bringing with him the Bishop and the Viceroy. They had great ceremonies there, with solemn Vespers on that evening, sung by the Viceroy's own choir, and next morning Pontifical High Mass, followed by a sermon preached by Fr. Gonçalo, with more than usual fervour and devotion. In the afternoon baptism was solemnly administered to forty-five converts, preceded and

[1] *Diversi Avisi dell' Indie*, &c. fol. 284.
[2] Polanco (*Chron. Soc. Jesu* vi. p. 788) says the 18th but the date is explicitly given in *Diversi Avisi* ... fol. 286. The point, however, is of slight consequence.

followed by a procession through the town, in which all the Christians of the district took part. Fr. Gonçalo was immensely impressed by the fervour displayed by these new converts to the faith. Before he left he permitted the Blessed Sacrament to be reserved in the church. This had not been done up to that time, for fear of the heathen depredations. He did the same at Bassein, in the church attached to the Jesuit College. At this latter place, Fr. Gonçalo remained until the end of December, preaching, catechizing, and settling the affairs of the Society. On the first day of the new year, 1557, he set out from Bassein, after preaching an eloquent sermon that morning in honour of the feast of the Holy Name. The objective of his journey was Cochin, situated in the south of India, on the Malabar coast. News had lately come from there of an heretical Armenian Bishop, who had left his native Cairo, and was spreading the poison of his disbeliefs amongst the native Christians. Fr. Melchior Carneiro had already proposed to hold with him a disputation at Cochin, but the Bishop had thought fit at the last moment to fly into the mountains of the interior. And recently the life of Fr. Carneiro himself had been attempted in the very streets of Cochin.

Some while after his arrival, Fr. Gonçalo found, attached to the tabernacle door of the Jesuit church, a paper containing blasphemies against Jesus Christ and His saints, and insults and abuse directed against himself. Suspicions being aroused, it was presently discovered that amongst the congregation were a number of pseudo-Christian Jews, who, whilst ostensibly practising the Catholic religion, were in reality spreading secretly the errors of their sect. In the following year, it may be here noted, the heretical Bishop was taken into custody, and though publicly renouncing his heresies, was transferred for safety's sake to Goa, and thence to Portugal.[1] Fr. Gonçalo remained at Cochin until the September of 1557, when

[1] There exists, or once existed, a book attacking the errors of the Abyssinians which was attributed to the pen of Fr. Gonçalo. The book is referred to in a letter, written probably by Fr. Luis de Azevedo, from Abyssinia, July, 1613. Fr. Beccari gives a short analysis of the contents of the letter, and thus refers to the book: "Libro attribuito al padre maestro Gonçalo de Sylveira, che entrò in Etiopia quand' era vicerè dell' India Francesco Barreto. Attacca a fondo gli errori loro. I frati lo travisarono e, per istanze di costoro, l'Imperatore lo proibì." (Beccari, S.J., *Rerum Æthiopicarum Scriptores Occidentales*, vol. i. p. 124.) The book, if by Fr. Gonçalo, would probably have been written in this year, 1557.

an outbreak of disease at Goa summoned him to the capital.

It was only in the November of this year that the news reached India of the death of St. Ignatius of Loyola, who had breathed his last on the 31st of July, 1556. Though this news was somewhat belated, the Provincial ordered a Solemn Requiem to be sung at the College of Saõ Paulo. The ceremonies were conducted with due magnificence, in the presence of the Viceroy and all his court, the Patriarch of Ethiopia officiating.[1]

It was also about this time that Dom Francisco Barreto, returning victorious from his second campaign against Ali Adil Shah, the sovereign of Bijapur, was persuaded by Fr. Gonçalo and his "Socius," or assistant, Fr. Francisco Rodriguez, to turn his attention to the question of the native Christians. As has been already said, the lot of these converts was rendered very hard by the indifference, or even hostility, of the Portuguese. Owing chiefly to the untiring exertions of the Jesuits, the condition of these poor unfortunates was greatly improved. Dom Francisco decreed that in Goa at least the

[1] See the account in Bartoli, *L'Asia*, vol. vii, pp. 8 and 9.

public practice of heathen cults be forbidden; that the native Christians should enjoy equal rights with the Portuguese, and that the public offices of the State should be given to Christians in preference to Brahman or Moor. It was surprising to note the increase in the number of converts as a result of these and similar measures. Fr. Rodriguez, on coming to India, had expressed the hope that the baptism of converts at the College of Saõ Paulo should number, on an average, at least one a day. In spite of their fewness in former years, they now far exceeded the estimate of Fr. Rodriguez. During the year 1557 the number of native conversions was reckoned at over 1,080;[1] whilst by the end of the year following, the baptisms had increased to 1,916.[2] In 1559, the last year of Fr. Gonçalo's Provincialate, the number is given as over 3,233.[3]

Still, the above extraordinary results secured at Goa must not be attributed to Fr. Gonçalo to the exclusion of those other workers, who were bearing in their own degree the burden and the heats of the day. Much of the Provincial's time was necessarily

---

[1] Sacchini, *Hist. Soc. Jesu*, part ii. lib. i. n. 146.
[2] *Ibid.* part ii. lib ii. n. 169.
[3] *Ibid.*, part ii. lib. iii. n. 124.

spent in visiting the houses and missions of his Province: though the duties of his office did not hinder him from his favourite occupations of constant preaching and works of mercy. Whilst pleading necessity as his excuse, he even confesses to having exceeded the limits in this respect imposed upon him before his departure for India by Fr. Miguel de Torres, the Provincial of Portugal. The tendency of Fr. Gonçalo to excess had not been forgotten by his Superiors at home: and to Fr. Francisco Rodriguez had been entrusted, amongst other cares, the superintendence of the health of his Provincial. Thus he was saved from many occasions of indiscretion into which his enthusiastic temperament would otherwise most probably have led him.

Nevertheless, Fr. Gonçalo found plenty of matter in which he might exercise his zeal and energy. Amongst other regulations, he prescribed that the Scholastics at Goa should add an extra hour in the evening to their usual daily meditation. For the Fathers engaged in missionary labours upon the Fishery Coast he instituted the practice of a reunion, to take place four times a year. At such meetings they would live for a few days the ordinary community life, confessing and doing penance for their faults, consulting or correcting one another, renewing their vows, and in general preparing themselves afresh for the work of the missions.

In the spring of 1558, Dom Francisco Barreto was succeeded as Viceroy by Dom Constantino de Bragança, who also showed himself a great friend to Fr. Gonçalo and the Jesuits. In the January of the following year an expedition set out under the new Viceroy against the town of Daman, some seventy miles to the north of Bassein, or nearly 100 miles to the north of what is now Bombay. This town had been ceded to the Portuguese some while ago by the King of Cambaia, but its Moorish or Abyssinian garrison (one is about as bad as the other, says Bartoli,[1] excusing his ignorance on the point) had as yet refused to surrender it. Accompanying the expedition, besides some Dominican and Franciscan Friars, were two Jesuits, Fr. Gonçalo da Silveira and Fr. Alberto de Araujo. The garrison fled upon the approach of the Portuguese, and the Viceroy, without the need of a single blow, was able to enter the town in triumph. Fr. Gonçalo's first act was to erect a number of crosses in the squares of the town, as trophies of the Christian victory. Meanwhile, the Viceroy was anxious that a Mass should be offered up

[1] *L'Asia*, vii. p. 136.

at once in thanksgiving. But on inquiry it was found that the priests, anticipating a hard day's work amongst the wounded, had already broken their fast. Fr. Gonçalo alone had declined to share their meal. Now, when the need for Mass was urgent, the messengers of the Viceroy were directed to him. Using the privilege granted to the Indian missionaries, he purified and consecrated the chief mosque of the town; and then, with the whole army as congregation, offered up the most holy Sacrifice of the Altar. Next day a High Mass was sung: and on the feast of the Purification, Fr. Gonçalo preached to an enormous concourse of people. Then it was that in gratitude for the services rendered, Dom Constantino presented Fr. Gonçalo, in the name of the King his master, with the church which now for the first time had echoed with the voice of a Catholic priest. The gratitude of the Viceroy for his bloodless victory found further expression on his return to Goa, when at the suggestion of the Provincial a magnificent church was built in thankoffering. It was dedicated to St. Thomas, the "Apostle of India," and the bones purporting to be those of the Saint were transferred, either now or very shortly afterwards, from Meliapor to an honoured sanctuary in this new church.

It was at Meliapor (now a suburb of Madras) that St. Francis Xavier, that other Apostle of the Indies, had spent so many nights in prayer and conflict before the little shrine of his earliest predecessor.[1] And the transference of the bones of St. Thomas aroused many memories also in connection with St. Francis which would be especially dear to one who had so recently succeeded him in the office of Provincial of India. Fr. Gonçalo had always a deeply-rooted veneration for that model of the modern apostle. It is interesting to note here a comparison between St. Francis and Fr. Gonçalo which was made by Fr. Melchior Nuñez, a former Provincial, and one who had known both intimately—a comparison which, while asserting the superiority of the canonized Saint, offers also its tribute of unequivocal praise to the latter. Asked his opinion as to the respective merits of the two, Fr. Nuñez replied: "Well, Fr. da Silveira was a saint, and we all know it. There's no one who doubts that. But in comparison with him, Master Francis is like an architect as distinguished from a common

---

[1] Coleridge, S.J., *Life and Letters of St. Francis Xavier*, i. pp. 296-7. For account of the relics of St. Thomas, see Maffei, *Historia Indicarum* (Lyons, 1589), lib. viii. p. 191. Cf. Bartoli, *Degli Uomini e de' Fatti, etc.*, iii. p. 201.

bricklayer."[1] God knows where *we* should come in as a third term in such a proportion!

Many biographers here relate an incident in connection with the building of this Church of São Thomé, which, if not necessarily miraculous, is at least evidence of an extraordinary profusion of God's grace. It is said that, though workmen of almost every creed were engaged in its structure, yet all without exception embraced the religion of Christ.

Fr. Gonçalo had now for three years fulfilled the office of Provincial of India. The letters from Portugal which arrived at Goa in the August or September of this year, 1559, included one from Fr. Laynez, the General of the Society of Jesus, appointing Fr. Antonio de Quadros as successor to Fr. Gonçalo. This Fr. de Quadros, it may be remembered, had been the Provincial when Fr. Gonçalo arrived in India in 1556. But he had only governed for some six months, having been chosen as Provincial by the Fathers in India until such time as the General should send them a Superior from Europe. In spite of the zeal and energy which during these three years Fr. Gonçalo had displayed, he was not however universally considered as a successful

[1] Bartoli, *L'Asia*, iv. p. 160.

Superior.[1] Here once again his fervour had sometimes overstepped his prudence; and on occasion the severity of his own ideal was apt to intrude somewhat roughly and unnecessarily upon the lowlier ideals of many of his subjects. The commonsense of Fr. Gonçalo frankly acknowledged such defects. Indeed, he was wont to enumerate, amongst the graces which God had bestowed upon him, the fact that his character was unsuited for the task of government.

Having handed over the reins to his successor, Fr. Gonçalo retired for a few months to the Noviciate at Goa. He had already given up any books, &c., which as Provincial he had deemed to be necessary: and even had exchanged his Breviary for one more shabby and dilapidated still. At the Noviciate his longing for the promised gift of a martyr's death found expression in the increased austerity of his life. His reading was mostly confined to St. Thomas Aquinas, and he dwelt especially on that part in which the saintly Dominican treats of the excellence of martyrdom. But his solitude was soon broken in upon by the news of fresh work to be undertaken in the vineyard of the Lord.

[1] Cf. Alegambe, *Mortes Illustres, &c.* i. p. 27.

IV.

An African Harvest.

Across the Pacific, in the country which now is known as Portuguese East Africa, but which in those far days was scarcely known at all, a cry had risen up to Heaven for the Word of God. A Dominican Friar, passing through Mozambique on his way to India to assume the duties of Bishop of Cochin, had heard the call; but, unable by his position to answer it in person, he had consulted with the Viceroy, the Patriarch, and the Jesuits at Goa, with a view to sending missionaries to meet the need.

Africa, as we have already said, was almost an untraversed land in the days of St. Ignatius and the early Society. Indeed, for long afterwards, in some respects even unto our own days, the land of the Kaffir has been little more than a background of fiction and romance. Pedro de Covilham, an explorer, writing directions to his master, the King of Portugal, for those adventurers who should dare to follow in his track, cannot give very explicit information as to the geography of the African coast. He suggests that "when they should arrive in the eastern ocean, their best direction must be to inquire for Sofala and the Island of the Moon."[1] Evidently he forgets that the "eastern ocean" is not dotted over with information-bureaux! Nevertheless, there were certain facts relating to the country and its inhabitants which the voyager might have gleaned with some slight expenditure of trouble. It was known to the Portuguese who traded along the eastern coast that within the interior, in the country lying between the Limpopo and Zambesi rivers, a great kingdom—an empire, they imagined it to be—flourished under the sovereignty of the Monomotapa, or Paramount Chief of the Makaranga.[2] This tribe, which in these days inhabits the Victoria District and the country west of it, was a very large one, greater in numbers than any tribe now existing in South Africa. It was

[1] Quoted by the Hon. A. Wilmot, *Monomotapa (Rhodesia)*, p. 123.

[2] Called "Amakalanga" by the Matabeles, Zulus, &c. The singular form of this word is "Mukaranga." The language they speak is known as "Chikaranga;" though nowadays those Makaranga who live in Matabeleland generally speak Sindebele. It is curious that for most of the other "Mashona" tribes, the word "Mukaranga" has come to have the connotation of "coward." (*Vide* Fr. Biehler, S.J., ZAMBESI MISSION RECORD (October, 1908), vol. iii. pp. 463, 464.)

split up into several smaller tribes under separate chiefs, few of whom were more than loosely connected with their Paramount. For the central authority of the Monomotapa was at this period but nominal—rather a remnant of the past than a living actuality. About half a century after Fr. Gonçalo's death, this phantom empire broke up into three or four principal states, which in their turn by constant internecine wars grew weaker and weaker, until the whole country came under the control of the Chartered Company.

South of the Monomotapa's territory, in the country around Inhambane and Cape Correntes, was another division of the Mukaranga tribe, possibly a part of the former kingdom, but which had been forced by circumstances to take refuge amongst its Batonga neighbours. The head kraal of this tribe was at Otongwe, some three days' journey from the coast. Here the chief Gamba resided, whose cry had reached the ears and hearts of the Indian missionaries.

One of the younger sons of Gamba, in intercourse with the Portuguese traders who yearly travelled from Mozambique to Inhambane for the sake of the ivory and amber of those parts, gradually acquired the knowledge and the desire of the Christian faith. One year he returned with the traders to Mozam-

bique, and before the next season had arrived
he was baptized in the little Church of São
Gabriel, the Governor or "Captain" of
Mozambique standing as his godfather. The
following year he returned in the annual
trading-vessel to Otongwe, confirmed at least
in faith. And his enthusiasm presently
inspired his other brothers, especially the
eldest, to imitate the example he had set.
But the old chief, Gamba, would not hear of
his sons trooping off in a body to Mozambique. However, he despatched a messenger
to the Governor, Bastião de Sá, begging that
a priest might visit his country, and promising
that he would himself become a Christian.
The petition, as we have seen, was brought
to Goa by the Dominican Bishop, and was
responded to with eagerness by the Jesuit
Provincial.

Fr. de Quadros, the Provincial in question,
had ever entertained the greatest esteem for
Fr. Gonçalo. They had entered the Novitiate
at Coimbra about the same time;[1] they had
been professed together at San Roque in
Lisbon; and the years they had spent with
one another had served only to increase their
mutual admiration and respect. Fr. de

---

[1] Fr. de Quadros entered the Society some time in
1544. Cf. Franco, *Synopsis Annalium S.J. in Lusitania,*
(Augsburg, 1726), p. 11.

Quadros used to say that were an anti-Christ to set up his standard in the world, Fr. Gonçalo would be the man to withstand him.[1] So it is not surprising that when there was question of a missionary to be sent to South-Eastern Africa, Fr. Gonçalo should have been the chosen man. His zeal had been tested well, and tempered by hard experience. The desire, the ideal of his life, was well known to the Provincial. Add to this that the new Captain of Sofala and Mozambique was a kinsman of his, and would be likely—indeed, had promised—to favour the enterprise to the full extent of his power.

Thus was the blood-red standard of the Cross of Christ thrust, as it were, by God's most loving generosity, within the willing, eager grasp of His servant. As comrades on this perilous journey he had two fellow-Jesuits. One was Fr. André Fernandes, who some years previously had been sent by Francis Xavier to Rome to report upon the condition of the Indian Mission. He was in middle age, and consequently rather older than his future Superior, Fr. Gonçalo, who was only in his thirty-fourth year. His correspondence shows him to have been of a

[1] Tanner, S.J., *Soc. Jesu usque ad sang. et vitæ profus. militans* (Prague, 1675), Pt. I. p. 160.

peculiar character. He seems to have been somewhat garrulous, fond of expressing his own opinions and grievances, though in a quaint, humorous fashion. We may suspect that he was not always the most agreeable companion possible to his austere and more sombre-minded fellow-missioner. The third member of the company was a lay-Brother,[1] Br. André da Costa, an old soldier, who had joined the Society two years previously. His health was not of the best, and, as we shall see, the experiences of South Africa did little to improve it.

With these two companions, then, Fr. Gonçalo left Goa for Chaul towards the close of the December of 1559. He had already bidden good-bye to the Viceroy, who entrusted him with gifts and friendly messages for the Inhambane chief, and also for the Monomotapa. At Chaul they found the new Captain of Mozambique, Pantaleão de Sá, waiting for the arrival of his kinsman on board his vessel. All being ready, they weighed anchor on the 13th of January, 1560, and after leaving the Indian coast did not sight land again until February 2nd, the

[1] Du Jarric, *L'Histoire des Choses plus memorables*, &c. (Arras, 1611), p. 158, states incorrectly that Fr. Gonçalo's companions were both priests. His mistake has since been copied by others.

feast of Our Lady's Purification. It is said that by the end of the voyage the discipline on board ship had become rather monastic than naval. Litanies were said every day, and special prayers to the Mother of God, composed by Fr. Gonçalo himself. Every morning he would preach on some virtue of our Lady, whilst in the evenings he would assemble the sailors and speak to them of the feast of the following day. Except when necessity or duty summoned him, he was scarcely ever to be seen on deck. Even in the sweltering calm which they encountered near the equator, he refused to leave his narrow cabin. There he would pray, meditating for an hour, both morning and evening, according to the rule he had prescribed for the Scholastics of Goa. But in truth such meditations were but landmarks, as it were, in a day where all was prayer.

After varied experiences, of which not the least was the partial failure of the water supply, they at length sighted land on February 2nd, and on Tuesday, the 4th, they anchored off Mozambique. Fr. Gonçalo's first act was to go on bare feet to give thanks for the safety of their voyage at the shrine of Our Lady of the Ramparts—"*Nossa Senhora do Baluarte.*" They remained over a week on the island, guests of the Captain, Pantaleão de Sá, who treated them with every mark of consideration and respect. Their time was spent, as usual, in works of mercy, preaching, and hearing confessions. One of the coastal trading-vessels—"*Zambucos*," they were named by the Portuguese—was due to start on the 12th for its yearly expedition to Inhambane. Fr. Gonçalo decided to take passage in this boat, though the Captain had offered him the use of his own ship. This course of action scarcely met with the approval of his companion, Fr. Fernandes. "The Father," he writes,[1] "would not go to Sofala in the captain's ship, but in a zambuco where there is no room for a man to stand, sit, or lie down. And though I represented to the Father the hardship and danger of travelling in such a craft, it seems that his desire of finding himself in one was such that he still wished we should go in it; and I assure you, beloved brethren, that while in it I was always weary, for besides the want of room for any man to be comfortable, it tossed so that it increased the hardship." In fact, it

[1] Letter of Fr. Fernandes to the Jesuits at Goa, Otongwe, June 26, 1560. *Vide* Theal, *Records of South-Eastern Africa*, vol. ii. pp. 83–4. In this volume, Dr. Theal collects the letters written by Fr. da Silveira and Fr. Fernandes from Africa, printing them both in their original Portuguese and in English. References are to his English translation.

began to toss before they had left harbour. And as it was already past the monsoon, they encountered little else than wind and rain until they arrived at Sofala on the 11th of March, after a journey of twenty-seven days. To add to the discomforts of a boat where it was almost impossible to obtain shelter, the season of Lent commenced in the week after they had left Mozambique. Rice and beans were their staple food, and that in strictest moderation. "The Father and Brother," writes[1] Fr. Fernandez, "ate the rice and beans, but when I found that one basin (of the latter) was not sufficient for me I asked for two, because, as I said, I lost my appetite for rice." By the time they had reached Sofala, the lay-Brother, André da Costa, had broken down, having developed symptoms of asthma. As soon as this was noticed, Fr. Gonçalo forbade him to fast any more, and ordered him meat and whatever delicacies were possible under the circumstances. At Sofala, where they rested for five or six days, matters did not improve. The village was situated on low and swampy ground, on the northern bank of an estuary fringed with belts of mangroves. It was, perhaps, the most unhealthy spot along that

---

[1] *Ibid.*, *vide* Theal, *Records*, &c., ii. p. 84.

coast, a very hotbed of fever and dysentery. On the journey from Sofala to Inhambane, which it took over a week to accomplish, even Fr. Gonçalo, though naturally of an excellent constitution, broke down under the hardships. Fr. Fernandes alone was able to get about, perhaps as a consequence of that discreet regulation of diet which is usually connected with the immortal name of Oliver Twist. At length they reached Inhambane on March 26th, and landed with but little more to boast of than their bare lives.

Inhambane, however—a small settlement at the mouth of the river—was, unlike Sofala, one of the most healthy localities in south-eastern Africa. Some fourteen miles above the river bar was a Mohammedan village under its own sheik: but the Portuguese, during their yearly sojourns, kept apart, erecting temporary huts along the bank. It must be remembered that neither the Portuguese nor even the Mohammedans exercised any real control or authority amongst the native tribes. They lived on sufferance, not by right of conquest. Individuals, indeed, might gain the confidence of some chief, and thus might occupy a post of authority in some native kraal. There were Portuguese who had degraded themselves to the level of the savage, adopting their habits and their morals. But the kaffir refused to surrender his independence, and traded with the "Vazungu" (so he called them) as with equals.

IV. (*continued.*)

HERE, then, Fr. Gonçalo and his two companions disembarked. Fr. Gonçalo was raging with fever, in danger of his life. They had landed on a Thursday, and Fr. Fernandes waited for two days, in dread lest his Superior should die and leave him to face unaided the future difficulties. The sufferer himself has told us, in most reserved language, the manner of his recovery. "It pleased God," he writes to his fellow Religious at the College of Saõ Paulo,[1] "that on Saturday afternoon having a moderate fever and ague, I went to the foot of a tree, and returned without fever, and from that time I became convalescent and had no more seizures, and was even able to say Mass on Palm Sunday. . . ." As to whether Fr. Gonçalo attributed his improvement to more than natural agencies, we have no means of information. And the half-expressed hope of Sacchini[2] that this event should turn out to

---

[1] Letter from Mozambique, August 9, 1560. (*V.* Theal, *Records*, &c. ii. p. 95.)

[2] *Hist. Soc. Jesu*, part ii. lib. iv. n. 217. Cf. Bartoli, *Degli Uomini e de' Fatti*, iii. p. 206.

be miraculous seems incapable either of realization or of destruction.

On that same Saturday Fr. Fernandes, feeling that all danger was now past, resolved to set out alone for Otongwe. It was, in fact, the will of his Superior that he should not wait for his comrades, but should commence at once his apostolic labours. Fr. Gonçalo recommended him to travel in a native hammock, as was the custom of the Portuguese traders. But Fr. Fernandes preferred to go on foot. Taking four Kaffirs with him, he began his journey of some ninety miles, reaching Otongwe on the following Wednesday morning. The Kaffirs, he found, walked very quickly: and so as not to lose authority and respect he was obliged to follow their example. The experience was rendered more painful by the fact that his shoes began to pinch after the first few steps; and as the Kaffirs would not wait for him to remedy the evil, he was forced, he writes,[1] to walk barefoot all that day. That evening they reached a small and shady native kraal, where Fr. Fernandes was only too willing to stay and rest. Sitting down upon the ground, he pulled his breviary from out his sleeve,

[1] Letter from Otongwe, June 26, 1560. (*V.* Theal, *Records*, &c. ii. p. 85.)

with the intention of saying his Office. But a crowd soon gathered round to see the prodigy. By way of amusement, Fr. Fernandes began to make a noise with the book, by running his thumb quickly over the leaves. The result was a cry of wonder from the assembled Kaffirs, who believed the book to be alive. After a night's rest, afforded by the hospitality of the headman of this kraal, they journeyed on; and without further adventure or mishap they reached Otongwe early on Wednesday. Within a very few hours of his arrival, he began to feel feverish. Nevertheless, on the day following, which was Holy Thursday, he visited the chief and announced the speedy arrival of his Superior. Gamba was delighted at the news, and treated Fr. Fernandes with every mark of kindness. The fever grew rapidly worse, and the Father was forced to take to his bed—which in those parts seemed identical with the bare ground—where for some days he remained, with little else than water and indian corn on which to thrive. A mulatto, João Raposo by name, whose services as interpreter had been secured either at Sofala or at Otongwe itself, attended him in his illness. At times he would be visited by the sons of the chief, whom he would catechize as best he could. By the following Thursday (April 9th) he records a decided improvement. On that day "I asked him [*i.e.*, João Raposo] to order me a boiled chicken."[1] Henceforward his recovery was rapid.

Meanwhile the invalids at Inhambane were slowly regaining their strength. As soon as Fr. Gonçalo considered the journey feasible, preparations were immediately made, native hammock-carriers were hired, and the two Jesuits started on their way. In spite of some slight trouble with the natives whose services had been requisitioned and whose appreciation of the value of money or its equivalent increased with the length of the journey, the destination was finally reached on the 18th of April. "Seventeen days after my arrival the Father came here; he was weak and enfeebled with the journey and as soon as he arrived at this place dropped on the sand, wherefore they came to tell me he was there, and without being able to raise his head he spoke to me. We brought him something to eat and drink, and then carried him to the bank of the river, where he wished to spend the night; afterwards the brother André da Costa came in the same manner, and also a servant they had with them."[2] As this is the last occasion

[1] Theal, *Records*, &c. ii. p. 87.
[2] Letter of Fr. Fernandes from Otongwe, June

where reference to André da Costa need be made, we may notice here that having returned to the coast after Fr. Gonçalo's departure in order to recuperate, he was finally sent back to India in the following year. It seems clear that, veteran soldier though he was, the African climate and the hardships endured so patiently had utterly ruined his health.[1] His return to India ends that connection which has served to rescue his name from the dusty annals of the Society.

Fr. Gonçalo speedily regained his strength, and commenced at once the work for which he had offered his life. After delivering the complimentary messages of the Viceroy of India, he was welcomed with great warmth, and given a hut in which to dwell. Permission was granted to all the subjects of Gamba to accept the new faith of the *Muzungu* priest, and within a very short while the Chief and his three pagan sons were admitted into the fold of the Catholic Church. Previous to this ceremony, it was of course necessary that Gamba should separate himself from those " extra " wives, whom, as a pagan, he

---

[1] Sacchini, *Hist. Soc. Jesu.* part ii. lib. vi. n. 158. Juvency, however, in his *Epitome Hist. Soc. Jesu,* ii. p. 104. (Edit. Gandia, 1853,) asserts that he died amongst the Kaffirs.

had seen fit to espouse. These women were themselves baptized, together with the one whom Gamba henceforth acknowledged to be his lawful partner. Soon the whole family of the Chief, and many lesser chieftains followed the royal example. The Faith spread gradually beyond the confines of the kraal. Every day fresh converts were added, sometimes singly, more often in crowds. Fr. Gonçalo calculated that during his stay of some seven weeks at Otongwe, he had baptized about 450 natives. "I made a point of baptizing a large number together immediately, because these people resemble children, who like to act together and follow each other's lead. They also resemble children as far as any intellectual impediment in receiving the Faith is concerned, for none of them have any kind of idol or form of worship resembling idolatry."[1] Such is the opinion of Fr. Gonçalo, after less than four months' experience of Kaffir life. On the subject of the native religion and beliefs the two missioners were not in agreement. Fr. Gonçalo was optimistic. "They have a God whom they call *Umbe;* they recognize a soul which lives after death and is punished or rewarded

---

[1] Letter of Fr. da Silveira from Mozambique, Aug. 9, 1560. *Vide* Theal, *Records*, &c., ii. p. 93.

according as it is good or evil. . . ."[1] The longer experience of Fr. Fernandes appears to contradict flatly the opinion of the former.[2] Dr. Theal has ventured upon a statement which may possibly be accepted by some as an adequate explanation of these differences. Politeness, he tells us, requires a Bantu to agree to everything that is said. "No one of them ever denies the existence of a Supreme Being, but admits it without hesitation as soon as he is told of it, though he may not once have thought of the subject before."[3] From this habit of soft speech he infers that the baptism of these Kaffirs was a mere result of their polite acquiescence in the truths proposed to their belief. One question it may be permitted here to ask. Would politeness have afforded a sufficient motive to the chief Gamba, that he should put away his harem of women, and with them the hope of that future wealth, to be acquired by the

[1] *Ibid.*, p. 93. On the subject of the native religion, see two very able articles by Mgr. Le Roy in the *Revue de Philosophie* (Sept. and Oct. 1908). They have since been expanded into a book, *La Religion des Primitifs* (Beauchesne et Cie.).

[2] Cf. Letter of Fr. Fernandes to the Society in Portugal, from Goa, Dec. 5, 1562. (Theal, *Records*, &c., ii. p. 147.)

[3] Theal, *History and Ethnography of S. Africa before 1795.* (Sonnenschein, 1907), vol. i. p. 308.

barter of their female progeny? It is not necessary, of course, to admire the wisdom of Fr. Gonçalo's action in thus hastening the baptism of natives before he had the time to acquaint himself with their customs and manner of life. It seems clear that, at a later period, many of these Kaffirs grew tired of that restraint which Christianity would impose. But that Gamba was insincere in his profession of faith is scarcely probable. Fr. Fernandes records of the Chief that "he is a very good man for a Kaffir, but drinks more than I could wish; but the interpreter tells me that he drinks very little in comparison to other chiefs. ∴ . ."[1] It seems natural to suppose that the presence of the missioners, and the example of the Chief, inspired the people with an enthusiasm which decreased as the consequences of their action began to dawn upon their somewhat obtuse and slovenly minds.

However this may be, the labours of the two missioners were incessant. Day by day the natives flocked to Gamba's kraal, to be washed in the sacred waters. A church was judged necessary and the building was begun: everything seemed prosperous and hopeful.

[1] Letter of Fr. Fernandes to his Provincial, from Otongwe, June 24, 1560. *Vide* Theal, *Records*, &c., ii, p. 66.

"Here"—writes Fr. Fernandes—"is a large harvest for many labourers. And I cannot understand the motive of Fr. Dom Gonçalo, for I can never get anything from him, except that a Brother and myself are sufficient here, and another Father and a Brother on the shore. . . ."[1] Fr. Gonçalo, in fact, had already made up his mind, in spite of the protestations of his comrade, to leave Otongwe, and to visit as soon as possible the great Monomotapa. The limits of Gamba's kraal were too circumscribed to satisfy the holy ambition of this adventurer in God's service. He thought to convert an empire. Tales had long been floating over Europe, describing in gorgeous fashion the splendours of the "Golden Emperor." The minds of the Portuguese had conceived of the Monomotapa in accordance with European categories. The Kaffir chief had assumed the honours of a Western Emperor, whilst his clay huts had been converted by the brilliant imaginations of the story-mongers into gold-lined palaces. Fr. Gonçalo solemnly assures the General of the Society that the Empire extends to the Cape of Good Hope;[2] and relates many wonderful tales of Kaffir customs. He now

[1] Letter of Fr. Fernandes from Otongwe, June 24, 1560. *Vide* Theal, *Records*, &c., ii. p. 63.
[2] Cf. *Nuovi Avisi dell' Indie* (3rd part), fol. 115—118.

considered that the conversion of the Monomotapa would open the way to a triumphal progress of Christ's Cross throughout the length and breadth of Southern Africa. What hastened his departure was the fact that the zambuco, or trading-vessel, in which they had travelled from Mozambique had already taken in its return cargo, and was preparing to set sail again for the north. If he did not seize this opportunity presented to him, he would probably have to wait another year before he could leave the Inhambane country. This plan, as we have suggested already, did not commend itself to the judgment of Fr. Fernandes: and from the remark of the latter quoted above,—that he could never get a word from Fr. Gonçalo—it seems clear that Fr. Gonçalo had ceased to argue the matter with him. After a stay at Otongwe of some seven weeks in all, he said a last good-bye to his fellow-missioners, and started upon his journey to the coast.[1] It was in the month

---

[1] Want of space forbids us to relate the story of the Otongwe Mission after Fr. Gonçalo's departure. For an account of Fr. Fernandes' troubles there, how he gradually lost the respect of the natives through no fault of his own, how the Christian doctrine was finally forbidden to be taught, and how the missioner returned in 1562, a white-haired, sunken-eyed, and tottering invalid, to his companions at Goa, cf.

of June, in the midst of the African winter: Fr. Gonçalo was consequently saved from the recurrence of the malaria which had attacked him on a former occasion. He had the happiness of converting on his journey some Indunas whom he chanced to come across. They were of the Batonga race—a people who are distinguished, amongst other ways, from their Makaranga neighbours by the rite of circumcision, A son also of a Batonga chief—greater even than Gamba in power and authority—was attracted by his words, accompanied him to Mozambique, and was there baptized.

Godigno, *Vita P. Gonzali Sylveriæ* (Cologne, 1616), pp. 82—90; Sacchini, *Hist. Soc. Jesu*, part ii. lib. vi. nn. 158—160; Theal, *Records of S.-E. Africa*, vol. ii. passim; also his *History and Ethnography of S. Africa before 1795*, vol. i. pp. 312, 313.

V.

At the Court of the "Golden Emperor."

Of his voyage to Mozambique we have few, if any, details. We are told that his union with God grew more and more as the expected end drew nearer. A letter written to Laynez about this time displays his zeal, and the earnestness with which he looked forward to the labours in store for him. He speaks of himself as a "merchant-trader," one of God's commercial travellers—if we may thus modernize his phrase,—whose wares were neither gold, nor silver, nor ivory, nor amber, but the ever-living Gospel of Jesus Christ. Again, he speaks pregnantly of his spiritual experiences amongst the Kaffirs. "If one may speak from the experience which one has gained on the waters and amongst the hills, it is there that God hides the full measure and the sweetness of His divinity and His humanity—a measure and a sweetness which is in the spiritual keeping of such as choose there a dwelling and a repose unto the profit of the Redeemer."[1]

With such thoughts as these Fr. Gonçalo

[1] Sacchini, *Hist. Soc. Jesu*, part ii. lib. iv. n, 222,

pursued his voyage, and arrived without mishap at Mozambique, where he hoped to catch some vessel sailing for Quilimane and the Zambesi. It was not, however, until the middle of August that he was able to continue his journey. On the 19th of that month[1] he set sail, accompanied by six Portuguese, of whom one, Antonio Diaz by name, was to act as interpreter. Pantaleão de Sá, the Governor, had made every arrangement, and had entrusted his kinsman with presents for the Monomotapa, in addition to those which Fr. Gonçalo had already received from the Viceroy of India. The zambuco, then, travelled south; and at about 150 miles from Mozambique it encountered a cyclone which placed the little vessel in most imminent danger of destruction. Antonio Diaz and his companions had almost abandoned hope, when Fr. Gonçalo went forward to the prow, fell upon his knees, and with arms outstretched besought the Lord of the Tempests to abate His wrath: "*Domine, salva nos, perimus.*" Immediately, we are told, the winds ceased, the sun shone out, dispersing the clouds, and the vessel was in safety.

---

[1] Godigno, *op. cit.* p. 91. Sacchini puts the date at September 18th (*Hist. Soc. Jesu*, part ii. lib. iv. n. 222). Neither writer is very accurate in chronology.

It was, perhaps, in thanksgiving for this favour that he thereupon put in to shore, with the intention of offering up the Holy Sacrifice of the altar. They were off the mouth of the river Mafute [1] when the answer to the prayer was heard; so they ran up the river for a little distance, and then moored the zambuco to the bank. A portable altar which Fr. Gonçalo carried with him was quickly set up, and the mystic Sacrifice of Calvary was re-enacted, probably for the first time upon that desolate and pagan shore. It is recorded that the sun beat so fiercely upon the uncovered head of the celebrant as to blister his scalp and face. He refused, however, to apply any remedy, leaving it to nature to repair the injury.

After a rest of three days the travellers continued their voyage, and arrived at the mouth of the Quilimane, some 300 miles south of Mozambique. At that period the Quilimane was the northernmost mouth of the Zambesi, though now it is so no longer. Two other outlets there were to the south (besides many smaller streams), the Luabo and the Cuama. The whole delta, extending from the Quilimane to the Luabo, a distance

[1] The Mafute may be found on some old maps about half-way between Quilimane and Mozambique. It is difficult to identify it with any modern river.

of some 100 miles, was known to the Portuguese as the "Rivers of Cuama." Sailing up the Quilimane for a few miles, they came to a settlement upon the bank where Mingoaxane, a friendly Bantu chief, received them kindly. This chief, whose title is pompously and somewhat inaccurately given as "King of Giloa" (or Guiloa), was Mohammedan in name. But, as in the case of so many other of the natives along the coast, there remained little of Mohammedan doctrine or ritual beyond the right of circumcision. Mingoaxane was anxious that Fr. Gonçalo should promulgate Christ's Gospel amongst his people. But the latter was of opinion that the conversion of the Monomotapa was of more pressing importance; and that with the baptism of the Paramount Chief, the conversion of the lesser chieftains would be comparatively simple. So he promised Mingoaxane that he would return to his country as soon as he could. He then set sail again, intending to make for the Luabo mouth. But a storm prevented his passage, driving the zambuco into a little harbour where the voyagers remained for nearly a fortnight. At last they ventured out once more, and steered for the Cuama, which they reached without adventure. The territory of the Monomotapa was held to extend as far as the mouth of the Cuama. Here then, on entering the Makaranga country for the first time, the boat was stopped and Fr. Gonçalo, disembarking, offered up Mass for the success of his enterprise. The boat then proceeded up the river; and on the eighth day they came in sight of a collection of huts, forming one of the Portuguese trading posts, or out-Stations, where the gold and ivory of the interior was collected, previous to its being shipped to Mozambique and the Indian ports. During the voyage up the Zambesi, Fr. Gonçalo had lived apart. A sail had been rigged up, at his request, so as to cut off one end of the deck from the public view. Behind this he had spent his time in retreat and prayer, coming out once a day for his food—a handful of roasted grain and a cup of water. At the sight of the village, known even then by the name of Sena, the Portuguese hastened to inform their companion of their arrival. Fr. Gonçalo's soul was stirred at the thought that now in very truth his labours were to begin. Summoning the others to his side, he said a *Pater* and *Ave* aloud: then he addressed his dearest Mother, Queen of Heaven, placing the success of the expedition in her hands and in those of her Infant Son. Our Blessed Lady, as we shall shortly see, was not unmindful of the trust reposed in her.

One of Fr. Gonçalo's first acts, after disembarking from the zambuco, was to despatch a messenger to the Monomotapa, announcing his arrival, and begging for permission to proceed. As the Paramount's kraal was about 300 miles westward from Sena, the answer to the message was not received till some two months later.[1] Meanwhile, he devoted himself to the spiritual welfare of the Portuguese and others at Sena, who were certainly in need of a Catholic priest. Ten or fifteen Europeans were living there, and their morals, we are told, were little above the Bantu standard in point of decency. Before he left, Fr. Gonçalo had induced some, at least, of the Portuguese inhabitants to abandon their licentiousness, and to enter the lawful bondage of the Sacrament of Matrimony. Some 500 of their slaves were baptized, and Sena began to assume a

[1] Godigno (*op. cit.* p. 98), says that Fr. Gonçalo remained four months at Sena. As he only allows about three and a half months for the whole journey from the Zambesi mouth to the Monomotapa's kraal, a week of which was spent in ascending the Zambesi to Sena, it is difficult to reconcile these two statements. The kraal, he says (*ibid.* p. 97), was 600 miles from Sena! The account in Theal, *Records*, &c., ii. p. 119, gives the time as two months.

Christian appearance. About three miles from Sena lived a peaceful and kindly Induna—"King of Inhamior," as the Portuguese used to call him. Fr. Gonçalo would often walk over to this Kaffir kraal, and instruct both him and his family in the Catholic Faith. They were anxious to receive Baptism, but Fr. Gonçalo judged it more expedient to defer the matter. He felt that it was almost tempting Providence to baptize these Kaffirs, and then to leave them without help or guide in their new-found Faith. Moreover, he suspected that it would not be gratifying to the Monomotapa, and consequently that it would imperil the success of his enterprise, were the latter to learn that he had been anticipated by one of his subjects in the reception of this Sacrament. Accordingly he promised the Induna, as he had already promised Mingoaxane that he would soon return and satisfy his desires. Much time during these weeks, as we may imagine, was spent in prayer and preparation for the difficulties in store for him. At length the messenger returned, accompanied by Gomez Coelho, a Portuguese resident of Tete, and an intimate friend of the Monomotapa. Fr. Gonçalo had begged this man to come and visit him, seeing that he knew well the Chikaranga language, and could also give him much information as to the character and personality of the Paramount Chief.

Preparations being completed, the party set out for Tete, a settlement some 150 miles higher up the river. The luggage and other goods were sent up to Tete by boat. Fr. Gonçalo travelled overland on foot, bearing on his back the materials for saying Mass. At Tete more native carriers were engaged, and the party, leaving the river, struck southward, with the intention of following the course of the Mazoe valley.[1] Whether the Portuguese who had accompanied Fr. Gonçalo from Mozambique were still in his company we know not. Gomez Coelho, at any rate, did not travel with him beyond Tete. But a servant of some sort was with him, from whom much information was afterwards gathered by the Jesuits at Goa.[2]

---

[1] The route followed by Fr. da Silveira after leaving Tete, and even the precise locality of the Paramount's kraal, are not beyond doubt. For a description of the country, and of the probable route, see an article by Fr. E. Biehler, S.J., "Some Notes on the Munomutapa and his People," in the ZAMBESI MISSION RECORD, vol. iii. (October, 1908), pp. 460—465.

[2] Cf. Letter of Luis Froes from Goa, December 15, 1561, *vide* Theal, *Records*, &c., ii. pp. 119, seqq.

V. (*continued.*)

FOR about a hundred miles the party travelled southward, or south-westward, until they reached Luanze, a Portuguese out-Station situated midway between the Inyadiri and the Ruenya, and some twenty miles south-east of the Mazoe.[1] From Luanze the route lay rather westward. Thirty or forty miles further on they would pass Bocuto, another trading-station in the M'rewa District; and thence, after crossing the Mazoe valley at some distance above its junction with the Inyadiri, they would finally reach Masapa and the "Gates of the Kingdom" of the Monomotapa. Masapa was once a flourishing centre of Portuguese trade; and though now but a collection of ruins, in the days of Fr. da Silveira it stood guarding the long defile through the hills to the south of Mount Fura,[2] which formed in fact as well as in name the "Gates" of the Monomotapa's

[1] Luanze was in the country known to-day as the M'toko District, the habitat of the Mabudjga tribe. Fr. Hartmann, S.J., made an unsuccessful attempt in 1891 to start a Mission in this country.

[2] Named Mount Darwin by the explorer, Mr. F. C Selous, in 1889.

tribal district. The Chief was no friend of the Portuguese, and was jealous of any attempt on their part to explore his territory. At Masapa he made use of a Portuguese, Antonio Caiado by name, in order to protect himself from the intrusions of the Europeans. This Caiado was probably one of the class popularly known as "white negroes," whose skin indeed was white or half-caste, but whose manners and morals were rather those of a Zulu. This personage lived chiefly at Masapa, glorying in the pompous title of "Capitão das Portas,"—"Captain of the Gates." It was his duty to inform the Chief of the advent of any European at the "Gates," and not to allow the stranger to proceed further without the royal permission.

We do not know how long the journey took from Tete to Masapa. Various stories are told of adventures on the road, of the deep rivers he had to swim or ford, of the scarcity of food, of the interest excited amongst the natives at his appearance. At Mabate, a kraal somewhere along his route, he is said to have baptized all the inhabitants, prophesying that the Faith would never leave the district. This prophecy, we are told, had not been falsified, at least as late as 1675, over a hundred years after the event.[1] On Christmas Day he said his three Masses at another kraal in the immediate vicinity of Masapa. The next day, December 26th, he reached Masapa[2] itself, where he was received by Caiado on behalf of the Monomotapa. The Chief had sent him such gifts as he thought would be welcome to the Portuguese stranger—gold-dust, oxen, and some female slaves. Fr. Gonçalo courteously refused to accept anything, saying that he did not seek the gifts of the Chief, but the Chief himself. At this news the Monomotapa seems to have expressed great surprise. It was not customary for a Portuguese to refuse such presents, especially the last. This circumstance evidently increased the Chief's opinion of the greatness and authority of his visitor; and he

[1] Tanner, *op. cit.* p. 160. One may doubt whether Fr. Tanner ever verified his statement, and did not merely copy verbatim from Godigno, *Vita P. Gonz. Silveriæ.* (Cologne, 1616), p. 101.

[2] The biographers confuse the trading-station of Masapa with the kraal of the Monomotapa. Hence they state that Fr. da Silveira arrived at the *kraal* on December 26th. Two head kraals, or "Zimbaoes," are mentioned in the *Records* (i. p. 23; iii. p. 356; &c.) —one near Masapa itself, and the other at N'pande, in the Beza-Chidima district. The Monomotapas would move from one locality to the other, according to the season of the year. (Cf. Hall, *Pre-Historic Rhodesia*, p. 109, n. 2.) At the time of Fr. da Silveira's visit, the

was eager to hold the promised interview. Fr. Gonçalo thus set out from Masapa, with Caiado as his companion and guide; and travelling north-westward arrived at the Chief's kraal after a journey of some three or four days. This kraal was situated upon the banks of the Musengezi, a river rising among the M'vurgwi hills to the south-west of Mount Darwin, passing at a distance of some forty miles from Masapa, and emptying itself into the Zambesi about fifty miles below the old Portuguese station of Zumbo.[1] The kraal itself must have been little more than forty or fifty miles from the junction: but since the Kaffir shifts his dwelling-place every few years—when the accumulation of dirt and vermin becomes intolerable even for him—we must not be surprised to find no traces left to tell its tale.

We may imagine that the expectations formed by Fr. Gonçalo as to the magnificence of the "Emperor of Monomotapa" and his Court fell short of actual realization. The

[1] There seems to be no doubt but that this is the river called by Fr. Godigno (*op. cit.* p. 110) the Mosengesses or Motetes. The alternative name may be accounted for by the fact that the Musengezi is said to change its name nearer its source, where it is known as the Utete. The doubt, however, as to whether these two form one river is not yet quite cleared up.

"royal palace" would on inspection prove to be a number of ordinary pole and grass huts; whilst the worthy "Emperor" would be transformed into a dirty and half-naked native Chief. It was not exactly what he had been led to anticipate: and it would be small wonder if even *his* enthusiasm was a little damped. However, his conversations with Coelho and Caiado, and still more his own experiences of Africa, would doubtless have prepared him in some degree for this meeting. At all events, he was not the man to lose heart. The Chief received him with evident delight, and accepted some cloth which Fr. Gonçalo presented to him. An interview took place in the Chief's own hut, into which not even Caiado was privileged to enter. Fr. Gonçalo sat on a mat between the Chief and his mother, whilst Caiado, standing in the doorway, acted as interpreter. The Chief questioned him closely as to how many wives he wanted, how many head of cattle, how much gold, and how much land. And again the missionary replied that he despised such things, and had come so far, not for any sordid love of gain, but for the glory of God and for the salvation of the Chief's own soul. These motives were a little beyond the comprehension of "his majesty," but the general effect was excellent; and after renewed offers of service, the interview came to an end, Fr. Gonçalo retiring to a hut that had been prepared for him in the kraal.

So far the prospects of success in this arduous undertaking seemed very promising to one who in his enthusiasm had little thought of analyzing the varied motives that must have swayed the Monomotapa in his friendly action. At this very moment his sovereignty was being fiercely contested by his half-brother, Tshepute, in revolt against him. In such circumstances it would scarcely be surprising that he should hesitate to annoy the representative of a power which alone was likely, or indeed was in the position to safeguard his supremacy by force of arms. Yet this probable admixture of motives does not exclude the presence of more honourable reasons for receiving Fr. Gonçalo with such favour. The young Chief was inquisitive. He had formed a high opinion of his visitor's uprightness and disinterestedness: and his wonder and admiration were increased by the events of the next few days.

Fr. Gonçalo had erected his altar in the hut that had been allotted him, and there every morning he said his Mass, served apparently by his servant. A few days after his arrival, as he was saying Mass, one of the lesser Chiefs was passing the entrance of the hut. Peeping in, he caught a glimpse of what he took to be a beautiful woman, standing in front of Fr. Gonçalo. Hastening to the Monomotapa he informed him that the visitor had brought with him a woman, lovely beyond description, who shared the dwelling of the *Muzungu*. The Chief presently sent a messenger to Fr. Gonçalo, begging to be allowed to see the woman of whose beauty he had heard, and whom he presumed to be his wife. The holy missioner was naturally a little astonished to receive a request of such a sort. But he soon grasped the situation, when the messenger pointed to a large picture of our Lady—"*Nossa Senhora da Graça*"— hanging behind the altar, as the wife in question. This was Fr. Gonçalo's opportunity, for which he rendered fervent thanks to Heaven. Wrapping the picture carefully in some rich cloth, he carried it to the Chief's hut. Before displaying it, however, to the eager eyes of the Monomotapa, he said a few words in explanation. He spoke to him of a God, the rewarder of good and the avenger of evil, who, to save us from ourselves and to win for us a future happiness, had come down from the heavens and had clothed Himself in the soft, gentle flesh of an immaculate Mother. Here, he said, was the representa-

tion of that holy Virgin, the spouse of the
Holy Spirit. And drawing aside the covering,
he knelt down in homage before the picture.
The Chief was enraptured at the sight, and
could scarcely turn his eyes away from it.
He begged his visitor again and again that
the picture might be left in his hut. So
Fr. Gonçalo left it with him, making a shrine
for it as best he could. After the death of
Fr. Gonçalo the story was told how for five
successive nights the Mother of God had
appeared in living form to this African Chief,
speaking words in a tongue unknown to him
or to his chieftains. At length he spoke to
Fr. Gonçalo on the subject, lamenting his
incapacity of understanding the language of
the vision. The missioner replied that they
alone could understand whose souls had been
cleansed in holy Baptism. The Chief was
silent. But two days later he informed
Antonio Caiado that he and his mother were
willing and anxious to join the Christians in
their worship. This was good news indeed.
Fr. Gonçalo, however, waited a few weeks
before baptizing them, in order that he might
instruct them in the rudiments of Catholicism.
At length, towards the close of January,
" within twenty-five days, a little more or
less,"[1] of the missioner's arrival, the Mono-

[1] Letter of Luis Froes, from Goa, December 15,

motapa and his mother were received within the bosom of the Church. That was a happy day for Fr. Gonçalo. How his heart must have swelled with gratitude to God and to His Blessed Mother as he poured the saving waters over the head of his royal neophyte! Here was the first great step in the conversion of a kingdom, of a continent. The prophetic words of Isaias would ring again in his ears: "And I will make my mountains a way, and my paths shall be exalted. Behold, these shall come from afar, and behold, these from the north and from the sea, and these from the south country. Give praise, O ye heavens, and rejoice, O earth ... because the Lord hath comforted His people, and will have mercy on His poor ones."[1]

For awhile his dreams were allowed to remain undisturbed. The name of Sebastião had been given to the Monomotapa, and that of Maria to his old mother. To celebrate the happy event, the Chief presented Fr. Gonçalo with 100 head of cattle. These Fr. Gonçalo at once handed over to Caiado to be slaughtered, and to be distributed in charity amongst such of the poorer natives as should come and ask for food. Caiado would have found little difficulty in disposing of this large quantity, even if we suppose that that

[1] Isaias lix. 11—13.

"white negro" did not consider himself to be an especially worthy object of charity. Generosity is *not* a peculiar virtue of the Kaffir: but he is always willing to accept of presents. This action of Fr. Gonçalo was therefore viewed with amazement, and added almost indefinitely to the esteem in which the Paramount held him. It was not long before some 300 of the more important natives around the Monomotapa's kraal followed their Chief's example, and after a certain amount of instruction, were received into the Church. The customary presents of milk, and butter, and eggs, and suchlike were made. These, too, Fr. Gonçalo distributed amongst the natives. For himself, he lived content on millet, cooked with herbs, and some bitter fruit which grew wild in those districts. His example, almost as much as his words, contributed very largely to the temporary success of his apostolic mission.

VI.

The Sacrifice.

IT may be remembered how at Coimbra, and again at Lisbon, Fr. Gonçalo had predicted both the fact and the manner of his future martyrdom. Needless to say, the idea of martyrdom had never faded from his mind. He had nourished it by prayer and meditation. He had lived a martyr's life. Now it was that the desire of his heart was to be given to him, his prediction to be verified. He was to die a martyr's death.

Almost from time immemorial Mohammedans from Arabia and Persia had been living along the East African coast, trading with the natives, mixing and intermarrying with them, sometimes converting them to their own religion. Francis Xavier had found them at Mozambique, at Melinda, and at Socotra. They had made their way inland from the coastal districts, and on his arrival at the Monomotapa's kraal, Fr. Gonçalo found a few who had penetrated into the very heart of the Makaranga country. By course of intermarriage with the Bantu, these Arabs had become scarcely distinguish-

able from the natives around them, save for
the turban and loin cloth which they always
wore, together with some sort of weapon.
The Mohammedans of rank, however, adorned
themselves in gorgeous robes of velvet or
other material, with sandals to their feet, and
an ornamented scimitar at their waists. One
of these latter, Mingane by name,[1] a *Caciz* or
Mohammedan priest who had recently come
up-country from Mozambique, showed himself particularly hostile to the Christian
missionary. He and three others of his kind
set themselves to destroy the reputation of
Fr. Gonçalo in the mind of the young Chief.
They represented to him that this would-be
Christian priest was in reality a spy sent by
the Governor of India or the Captain of
Sofala to report upon the precise locality of
the gold-mines, and upon the defences of his
kingdom. At other times they would insinuate
that he was a confederate of Tshepute, the
rival of the Monomotapa; that he was a
"Muzungu"[2] wizard, or "Muroyi," as the

---

[1] The name is variously given as Mingames, Mingoanes, or even as Aligamus. (Wilmot, *Monomotapa*, Append. C. p. 241.)

[2] Muzungu (pl. Vazungu) means "white man," and was used chiefly to designate the Portuguese, and the "white negroes." The word may thus have conveyed a contemptuous sense.

natives use the term; that his liberality towards the natives was an attempt to estrange them from their rightful ruler. By these and other arguments of a similar nature they worked upon the credulity and passions of the young Paramount, whose character, superstitious and fickle like that of most of his race, easily lent itself to such influences. Perhaps, too, the restraints of Christianity were beginning to prey upon the mind of this convert of a month's standing. Certain it is that he lent a ready ear to these suggestions of evil. But Fr. Gonçalo was not ignorant of the intrigues that were in progress. Before the treachery of the Arabs was thought to be known to any but themselves and the Chief, he remarked one day to Antonio Caiado: " I know that the Chief will kill me, and I am delighted to receive such a happy end from the hand of God."[1] Caiado was incredulous. "It is

---

[1] The following account is taken chiefly from the letter of the Jesuit scholastic, Luis Froes, dated December 15, 1561, which collects most of the information as to the manner of Fr. Gonçalo's death. Two letters of Fr. Gonçalo, however (one to Fr. de Quadros at Goa, and the other to the Captain of Sofala), written a few days before his death, were entrusted to Caiado: but, according to the latter's account, they were both lost at sea. Those who suspect Caiado of duplicity may find in this fact fresh confirmation of

impossible," he replied, that " the Chief should do such a thing, seeing that he is such a friend to your Reverence." Yet the remark troubled him: and soon after he went to the Monomotapa, to learn the real truth of the matter. The Chief made no secret of his intentions. He advised Caiado, if he had any property in Fr. Gonçalo's hut, to remove it at once, since he was going to order the death of the missionary. Caiado expostulated: but he could not deter the Chief from his purpose. So he hurried off to Fr. Gonçalo, and related to him all that had occurred. A little later he renewed his attempt to allay the suspicions of the Chief: and this time he thought to have gained a point. For the Chief informed him that the most he would do to Fr. Gonçalo would be to banish him from his country. This was on a Friday, the 14th of March. On the next morning a council was held, at which the Chief's mother and the Mohammedan *cacices* were present. It was there decided that Fr. Gonçalo should be done to death that very night. During the course of the morning Caiado visited the mother, hoping to be able

their views. The whole conduct of this "white negro" is certainly open to suspicion. But the evidence is quite insufficient on which to accuse him of being either an accomplice or an abettor of the murder of Fr. da Silveira.

to win her over to his side. But that astute old lady was now as bitter an enemy of Fr. Gonçalo as were the Arabs. To save appearances, however, she gave Caiado to understand that the decision of the council was that Fr. Gonçalo be banished from the Monomotapa's country. She promised to interview the Chief next day and intercede with him on behalf of the missionary; knowing full well, of course, that the next day would never dawn for Fr. Gonçalo. It is clear that Fr. Gonçalo had no doubts as to his impending fate: he knew as well as the Chief himself that this day was the last that he would spend on earth. When Caiado returned from his interview with the Monomotapa's mother, he begged him to summon two or three Portuguese who were living somewhere in the neighbourhood,[1] in order that he might hear their confessions and give them Holy Communion for the last time. He waited for them until mid-day: as they did not

---

[1] Caiado would not have gone himself, but most probably would have despatched native runners. These Portuguese traders must have been living at Masapa, or probably nearer still to the Monomotapa's kraal. Though Caiado's headquarters were at Masapa, he was evidently living at this time in the neighbourhood of the kraal. His duties, &c., would often have rendered this convenient.

arrive, he said his Mass, consuming the Hosts that he had consecrated. That same day he baptized about fifty native neophytes whom for some weeks he had been instructing, presenting each of them with beads and cloth. The Chief was greatly annoyed when he heard of this, and ordered the cloth to be taken from them.

In the afternoon Caiado returned with the other Portuguese, and Fr. Gonçalo was at least able to hear their confessions, and to exhort them to the constant practice of their religion. On their departure, he committed to the care of Caiado the vestments, chalice, and other altar-furniture, together with a few personal effects. He kept in his hut only a crucifix and a couple of candles. When Caiado returned to him in the evening, he found him dressed in his cassock and surplice, walking up and down in front of his hut. Fr. Gonçalo turned towards him with a smile of welcome. "Antonio," he said earnestly, "I am sure that I am readier to die than are my enemies to kill me. I forgive the Chief, who is but a youth, and his mother, because the Mohammedans have deceived them." Then he prayed that his death might suffice to atone for the crime about to be committed. Caiado was still half incredulous, or at least expressed himself as such. Returning to his own hut, he despatched two servants with orders to watch the hut of Fr. Gonçalo and to report to him at once if they should notice anything amiss.[1] These servants performed at least one part of their duty well, namely, to keep a careful watch upon the hut of the missioner. They observed that he was restless and disquieted. For hour after hour he was to be seen walking up and down amongst the shadows in front of his hut. His steps were hurried and irregular. Often he would pause in his walk and pray aloud, lifting up his arms to heaven, or holding them in the form of a cross. At times he would re-enter his hut and prostrate himself before the crucifix. Then he would come out again into the open air, and continue his weary vigil. They heard him muttering to himself. At times they could even distinguish the words that he used. Now he was praying for his enemies, now he was begging strength

---

[1] These precautions, as Sacchini suggests (*Hist. Soc. Jesu*, part. ii. lib. v. n. 232) were utterly inadequate to the gravity of the situation. In the Vatican folio edition of the History of the Society, of which a portion is translated in Hon. A. Wilmot's *Monomotapa* (Append. C. p. 245), it is stated that Calado had arranged with Fr. Gonçalo a plan of flight. But in the common folio edition (published at Antwerp in 1620) there is no mention at all of such a plan.

to suffer patiently the martyrdom in store for him; or, again, he was accusing himself before God of his unworthiness. When it was almost midnight, he entered his hut once more; and placing the two lighted candles on either side of the crucifix, he knelt before it in prayer. It was not long before weariness overcame him, and laying himself upon his bed—a mat of plaited reeds—he fell asleep.

Meanwhile, other eyes than those of Caiado's two servants had been watching his movements. Eight Kaffirs, bribed by the Mohammedan *Caciz*, had been secretly awaiting a favourable opportunity for their evil deed. Their leader was Mocrume, a Kaffir who, though not a Christian, had professed himself a staunch friend of Fr. Gonçalo. In the silence of the night they had lain in wait, not daring to attack until the possibility of resistance had been removed. Then, after making sure that their victim is fast asleep, at a given signal, they rush to the hut. Their leader throws himself upon Gonçalo's chest. Others secure his arms and legs. A rope is quickly twisted about his neck. There is a sickening sound, half gasp, half choke—and all is over. His shining soul, unsheathed, in Dante's vivid phrase, from the body's scabbard—" dalla vagina delle membre sue "—

flashed to Heaven. The body lay upon the ground, the blood gushing from the nose and mouth.[1]

At this juncture, apparently, the servants of Caiado decamped. Whether their conduct was due to fright or to bribery, or to some other cause, we are left to ourselves to determine. On the following morning they were not to be found; and it was presumed that they were hiding somewhere in the immediate vicinity. At all events, the report of the murder soon reached Caiado's ears. For in the grey dawn of the Sunday morning, he despatched the servant of Fr. Gonçalo and another servant of his own to inspect the hut. Tracks of blood were to be seen at the entrance. The murderers had dragged the body from the hut, and thrown it into the Musengezi close by. This may possibly have been the ordinary mode of burial, as it

[1] Thus the death must have occurred in the first hour or so of Sunday morning, March 16, 1561. Owing to a curious mistake, explained by Godigno (*op. cit.* p. 120), the date of his death has been erroneously given as August 11th: see, for example, Ribadeneira, in *Vita P. Lainii*, lib. 2, cap. xi.; Du Jarric, *L'Histoire des choses plus memorables*, &c. (Arras, 1611), p. 173; Wilmot, *Monomotapa*, p. 174; Hall, *Pre-Historic Rhodesia* (Fisher Unwin, 1909), p. 456. In many places March 15th is the date ascribed. But it was almost certainly past midnight when the murder took place,

is amongst some other African tribes. Or, what is more probable, the Mohammedans had persuaded the Chief not to leave the body under the sun, lest the "wizard's" corpse should poison the air that they breathed.[1] It is said that before throwing the body into the river, the murderers had stripped it. And finding next to his skin a shirt of iron points, they mistook the instrument of penance for the protective armour of a sorcerer. Inside the hut was found the crucifix, sadly mutilated, before which the martyr had uttered his latest prayer. One arm was broken, the head and the nails were missing. Caiado, on being informed of the results of their investigations, made them return to bring him the broken crucifix. This he afterwards sent to a certain friend of his, one Gaspar Gonçalves by name, living in another part of the same country.

In this way the missionary enterprise upon which Fr. Gonçalo had set his heart ended in almost complete failure. Both at Otongwe and in the country of the Monomotapa the Christian religion had been received for a while, and then abjured, and its ministers persecuted. It has been laid to the charge of

---

[1] Cf. Godigno, *op. cit.* p. 120; Theal, *Records*, &c., ii. p. 104.

Fr. Gonçalo that his undue haste in baptizing the natives after only a few weeks' probation was the chief cause of the failure of his mission. We have already heard the justification by Fr. Gonçalo himself on his action in this regard. Undoubtedly in later days such action would be rightly considered as the extreme of folly. The Dominican Friars of the seventeenth century had reached the conclusion that is being acted upon at present by the modern Jesuit missionary in Rhodesia, that the hope of Catholicism amongst the natives lies almost exclusively in the little children.[1] "After a year of labour and toil in daily instructions," writes a Jesuit from Chishawasha, "we can hardly make an impression of the first principles of religion on *young* native minds, and none on old; what of baptizing some after a few days, others after a few weeks? No wonder of the after-effects!" Nevertheless we must bear in mind that Fr. Gonçalo was a pioneer with no experience, personal or otherwise, of the natives with whom he had to deal. Someone has said that amongst the earlier Christian missionaries the similarities of human nature always impressed them more than the differences. They appear in those days to have

[1] Theal, *History and Ethnography of South Africa before 1795*, vol. i. p. 464.

been only partially successful in entering into the difficulties and obscurations of the native mind. They were inclined to view man as a type, rather than as an individual. The impediments to Christianity were considered usually to lie in the perversity of the will, and very little in the incapacity of the intellect. Thus it was no uncommon thing, this practice of hasty Baptism. It had been done in Southern India by Miguel Vaz, the Vicar of the Bishop of Goa.[1] St. Francis Xavier tells us how in Travancore he had himself baptized more than 10,000 in the space of one month.[2] It is not, then, altogether surprising that Fr. Gonçalo should have followed in Africa the course that had been adopted so often in other countries. Doubtless he would have been more than justified, in this country at least, in striking out a new line of conduct for himself. Yet it is not wonderful that he did not do so.

Moreover, it must be remembered that the question of the wisdom or the imprudence of Fr. Gonçalo's conduct in this regard detracts nothing at all from his just claim to be ranked as one of the most intrepid missionaries of the Society of Jesus. In more recent

[1] Bartoli, *Asia*, t. i. lib. i. p. 49.
[2] Coleridge, S.J., *Life and Letters of St. Francis Xavier*, vol. i. p. 280.

years, the heroic expedition of Fr. Augustus Law from Bulawayo to Umzila's kraal is recognized on all sides to be one of the most wonderful and daring feats recorded in African ecclesiastical history. And yet Fr. da Silveira's journey to the Monomotapa's kraal, and his labours there are surely still more stupendous. For, in the former case, Fr. Law was provided for more than half his journey with the help and comforts which the possession of a well-stocked waggon entails. And above all he was not alone, but attended, even to his last breath, by his faithful comrade and fellow-Religious, Br. Hedley. But the earlier missionary was without such consolations. The only white companion on his long journey was a servant of some sort, whose later conduct, at any rate, is open to suspicion. Nor was his acquaintance with Caiado altogether an unmixed blessing. Furthermore, the comforts (one might well say the necessities) of meat and European diet were deliberately refused by him in favour of the millet and Indian corn of the natives. Truly, the heroism of Fr. Gonçalo can only be fully appreciated by such as have had experience themselves of the trials, the hardships, and the dangers, spiritual and temporal, of native missionary life.

VII.

Flotsam.

THE Monomotapa was not content with having murdered his benefactor. A day or two later he ordered the execution of the fifty converts whom Fr. Gonçalo had baptized the day before his death. Fortunately, however, the order was never carried out. It was pointed out to him by some of the chiefs who remained faithful to the religion they had embraced that if these converts were worthy of death, then it was just that all the Christians, including themselves, should suffer the like penalty. As the Monomotapa perceived that his chiefs had not the slightest intention of being executed themselves, his prudence suggested the reversal of the sentence. Meanwhile, the Mohammedans were rejoicing at the havoc they had wrought. But a famine that broke out, followed by a pest of locusts, was turned to good account by Caiado. He persuaded the Paramount that the vengeance of the Christian God was overtaking him and his people for the outrage that they had perpetrated. In dismay, the fickle Chief ordered the death of the Mohammedan Cacices. Two of them, it is said, were caught and killed; the other two, of whom Mingane was one, saved themselves by a timely flight.

But the cup of retribution was not yet full. A year or two after the events that have been related, the mother of the Paramount was herself, from some reason or other, put to death by order of her son. And in a few years the whole country was in dismay at the news of a Portuguese expedition that was advancing against them. The new King of Portugal, Dom Sebastião, had conceived the idea of making South Africa the rival of the El Dorado of the Spaniards. To ease his mind he consulted a "board of conscience," composed of seven or eight lawyers, as to the justice of making war. The decision, as might be expected, was favourable to the enterprise of the King. The object of the war was stated to be threefold: firstly, to spread the Gospel amongst the Kaffirs; secondly, to obtain gold for the support of the Portuguese Government in India; and, thirdly, to avenge the murder of their countryman, Gonçalo da Silveira. In 1569 a large expedition was fitted out, under the command of Dom Francesco Barreto, who had been Viceroy of India when Fr. Gonçalo arrived at Goa in 1556. It was not till November, 1571, however, that the fleet, sadly reduced in numbers, left Mozambique, and sailed up the Zambesi to Sena. There were several encounters with the natives, yet no very decisive action. But the Monomotapa took alarm, and despatched an embassy to Barreto with proposals of peace. Barreto replied that on three conditions he would make peace. The Mohammedans living in the country were to be expelled, the country was to be open to Christian missionaries, and a certain number of gold-mines were to be ceded to the Portuguese. The Monomotapa agreed to this: and though the last condition was never fulfilled, it seems that the two former, to some extent at least, were carried into execution. Certainly, by 1586, Dominican Friars were settled in the Makaranga country. They had established out-Stations at Masapa, at Luanze, and at Bocuto, which were visited periodically by a missionary from Tete. In 1590 there were four Jesuit Stations in South-Eastern Africa—at Mozambique, Quilimane, Sena, and Tete.[1] Owing, however, to rivalry between the Dominicans and the Jesuits, it was decreed in 1610 by the King of Portugal that the land south of the Zambesi should be left in the hands of the

[1] Cordara, *Hist. Soc. Jesu*, part vi. lib. i. n. 145.

Friars.[1] The Jesuits, therefore, were unable to establish out-Stations in the country: though their Missions on the Zambesi itself still remained under their control. In 1697, besides a Jesuit Mission Station at Tete, &c., we hear of a seminary at Sena, established for the education of the European children in that country, and for the sons of the Bantu chiefs. Great work was also accomplished by the Dominicans during a long period of trial and disappointment. In 1652 they had baptized another of the Monomotapas: but his conversion led to no important results. It was not, however, until about 1830 that the last Dominican left the shores of South-Eastern Africa.[2]

It remains to say something in connection with a remarkable story of the miraculous preservation of the corpse of Fr. da Silveira. Indeed, there were numerous legends relating to the martyr that had gained currency amongst the Kaffirs. There were tales of a wonderful light floating over the spot where the body of Fr. Gonçalo had disappeared beneath the waters of the Musengezi. The crocodiles of that river were said to have

[1] Theal, *History and Ethnography of South Africa before 1795*, vol. i. p. 455. Most of the above facts are taken from these pages.

[2] Wilmot, *Monomotapa*, p. 217.

lost their savageness, and never more to have injured man in any way. But the most marvellous legend of all was that reported by Fr. Alfonso Leo de Barbudas, whose sworn testimony cannot be too lightly set aside.[1] This Jesuit was sent by the Viceroy of India, Dom Luis d'Ataide, in the year 1625, to visit for some purpose or other the kingdom of the Monomotapa. Whilst travelling on the Zambesi (whether up or down stream is not quite clear) he arrived one evening at a place where an island in mid-stream separates the river into two channels.[2] Here he decided to remain for the night, since the

[1] "Cujus juratum testimonium est mihi longe gravissimum, licet de re ipsa nihil affirmare ausim," says Cordara. (*Hist. Soc. Jesu*, part vi. lib. x. n. 167.) Cordara then relates the story in his own words. The actual report of Fr. de Barbudas is given in full by Tellez, *Chronica da Companhia de Jesu*, etc. (Lisbon, 1645—1647), vol. ii. pp. 164—166.

[2] The place is said to be "haud longe ab Arce Tuife" (Tanner, *Soc. Jesu usque ad sang. et vit. profusionem militans* (Prague, 1675). Part i. p. 163.) The "Isle of Mozambique," situated at the western extremity of the Lupata Gorge, below Tete, may possibly have been the place referred to. Rugged cliffs rise up on either bank at the entrance of the gorge. That on the right bank is known by the name of Tipwi. (Cf. F. C. Selous, *Travel and Adventure in South-East Africa*, p. 273.) If this be the place, the corpse must have travelled a long way.

stream was very rapid, and he feared the perils of submerged rocks. So he moored his boat to one of the river banks. The island, he noticed, was densely wooded: and he was struck by the presence of a number of birds, of extraordinary beauty, perched upon a log that apparently had floated down the river and been thrown up onto the island. The birds seem to have somewhat resembled cockatoos in general appearance. They are described as being of a white colour, relieved by a little black upon their wings, with a large crest on their heads. The beak and legs were of a deep reddish tint. Their song he compared enthusiastically to "the sweet harmonious blending of voices of different quality." They cannot certainly have been cockatoos! Native fishermen whom he questioned reported that a fixed number of these birds was always perched upon the log; and that at regular intervals they were relieved from their guard by other birds of the same species. Fr. de Barbudas, it is said, observed this phenomenon for himself on the following day. Two or three young Kaffirs who had accompanied him on his journey proposed to land on the island and make a closer examination. But the fishermen dissuaded them, saying that the island was infested with tigers and other animals which would not allow any man to set foot within the wood. Then they told Fr. de Barbudas the following story. Long ago the body of a white man, dressed in the same kind of habit that Fr. de Barbudas was wearing, had floated down the river tied to a tree-trunk. The trunk had remained fast to the island, together with the corpse. A number of tigers had immediately issued from the undergrowth, and severing the cords that bound the body had dragged it into the wood, leaving the log on the bank. From that time the log had been constantly guarded by the birds which have just been described. These things, they added, had happened within living memory, some sixty years ago or more. It was a tradition that whoever had inhabited that body was a very holy man, since even the brute beasts paid homage to his corpse. One old fisherman related how, within his memory, a neighbouring chief had resolved to test the truth of the story. A number of natives had approached the island from one side, thus attracting the tigers to the spot. Meanwhile two natives landed on the opposite side, and posted themselves amongst the topmost branches of a high tree. From that position they were enabled to see a clearing in the middle of the wood, and in it the body of a man, dressed in black, surrounded by tigers that kept guard in turn, like the birds upon the log. They remained a whole day on the island, escaping by the same method of tactics as they had employed on the previous day. Fr. de Barbudas was convinced that this corpse could only have been that of Fr. da Silveira, whose memory had not yet died out in the minds of the natives, even in those distant parts of the country. Moreover, he seems to have placed implicit confidence in the truth of this story, narrated on second or third-hand evidence. Whether all or any of the essential features of this tradition are true or not we should not care to assert. It is a beautiful legend: and perhaps it were best to leave it at that. But it may be interesting to quote in this connection a passage from an old chronicler, written some years previous to the journey of Fr. de Barbudas. He refers to the attempt made by the Jesuit, Fr. de Monclaros, during the Portuguese expedition of 1569—1572, "to see whether he could find the relics of his (Fr. da Silveira's) bones; which was impossible, because all the men who carried on trade at that time in the lands of Monomotapa asserted that as soon as the body of this holy Father was thrown into the river it was immediately eaten and devoured by the iguanas and crocodiles. Therefore it could not reappear, excepting at the last universal judgment."[1] This most prosaic version of the story, apart from its inherent probability, is even less trustworthy as a piece of evidence than the narrative of the Kaffir fishermen. But we will take a hint from the pages of this old sceptic, and make no pretence of anticipating by our hasty judgments the day of Doom.

---

[1] Diogo de Couto, *Da Asia*, dec ix. ch. xx.: *vide* Theal, *Records*, &c., vol. vi. p. 362.

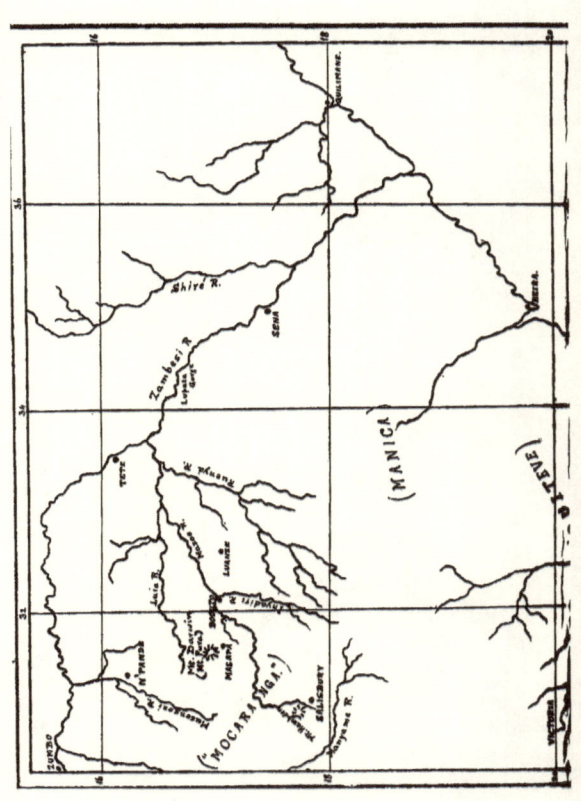

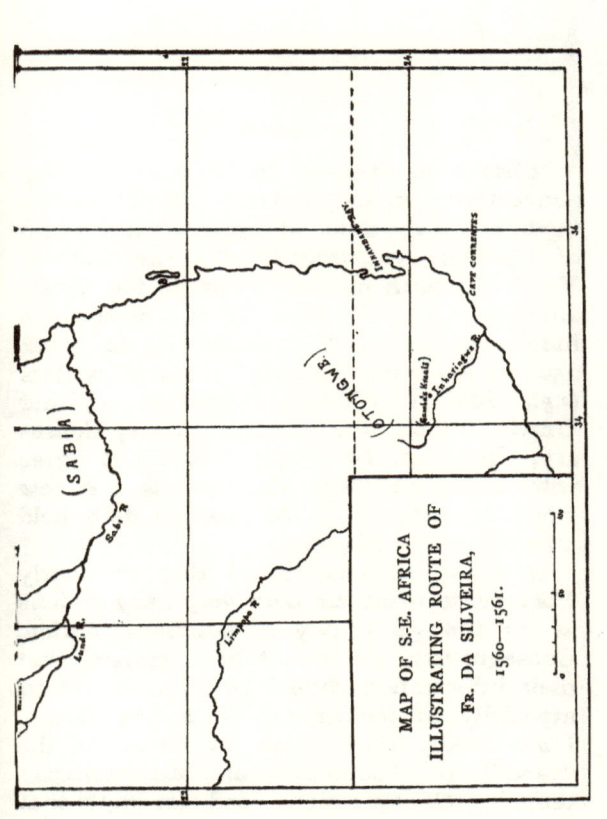

APPENDIX.

It has been assumed in the course of the above narrative, first, that the word "Monomotapa" is not the name of a place, but the title of a person; and, secondly, that the death of Fr. da Silveira occurred, not at the Great Zimbabwe, near Victoria, but at a place some hundred miles north of Salisbury, and over 250 miles from Victoria. Many writers (*e.g.*, Hon. A. Wilmot, *Monomotapa*—Fisher Unwin, 1896; and cf. *The Month*, February, 1909, pp. 151—155) would not agree with either of these assumptions. A few words in support of the position here held may not be out of place.

It must be remembered that the early Portuguese explorers held very hazy notions as to the geography of southern Africa. Consequently, we cannot be surprised that their information should be often incorrect, especially in the matter of native names. Undoubtedly they speak at times of the "land" or "country" of Monomotapa: though such expressions need not imply that Monomotapa is a land, but only that such land is in the possession of a person known by that name. De Barros, in his *Decades*, mentions "a vast country over which a prince named Benomotapa rules" (quoted by Mr. Wilmot, *op. cit.* p. 149). "Benomotapa," it may be noted, is probably a corrupted plural form of "Monomotapa," though De Barros did not know it. Again, the Dominican, Fr. Dos Santos, a most careful writer, tells us: "*The* Monomatapa and all his vassals are Mocarangas, a name which they have because they live in the land of Mocaranga. . . ." (*Records*, vii. p. 288.) These quotations may suffice as examples to show —what is now admitted in most quarters— that "Monomotapa" is the name (or title) of the ruler of the Makaranga tribe. The word itself is more correctly spelt by Englishmen as "Munomutapa," or "Munumutapa," since the English "u" represents to us the native vowel-sound, which by the Portuguese was identified with the nasal sound of the "o." The older spelling, however, is too well established to be changed. The word is said by Fr. Biehler, S.J. (ZAMBESI MISSION RECORD vol. iii. p. 463) to signify "you make him slave." Elliott's Chikaranga Dictionary gives the meaning as "the man who plunders." And in Theal's *Records* (vii. p. 202) we find the title "Great Thief" given by the Makaranga as one of the "praise-names" of their chief (cf. R. N. Hall, *Prehistoric Rhodesia*, p. 32, note). The word was used, somewhat similarly to our "Czar" or "Kaiser," as a permanent title adhering, not to any particular Mukaranga chief, but to the office or position which he held. A similar custom is carried on in our own days amongst the Washawasha tribe, whose Paramount Chief, whomever for the time he may happen to be, is known by the name of the Chinamora.

The question of the locality of the Monomotapa's head-quarters has been recently discussed by Mr. R. N. Hall in his *Prehistoric Rhodesia* (Fisher Unwin, 1909). And the fact is there clearly proved that in 1560 the Great Zimbabwe was not even within the territory of the Monomotapa's kingdom, but was included in the boundaries of the rebel kingdom of Sabia (or Sedanda). As has been already noted, the *Records of South-Eastern Africa* make mention of only two "Zimbaoes" of the Monomotapa. The one was near Mt. Fura (now called Mt. Darwin), not far from the Portuguese trading-station of Masapa. The other was to the north-west of Masapa, in the Beza-Chidima district, "close by" the Musengezi river. Near this latter kraal were some ancient ruins—ancient even in those days—of which "the Kaffirs say they are a supreme piece of work. All the 'Monomotapas' are buried there, and it serves them for a cemetery" (*Records*, iii. p. 356). This kraal in Beza-Chidima is stated to be "the common residence of the Monomotapa" (*ibid*. i. p. 15), though both this and the Zimbaoe near Masapa were in use, according to the season of the year. It may be worthy of notice that in the opinion of Mr. Hall (*op. cit.* pp. 116—118) the words "Zimbabwe" and "Zimbaoe" are totally different words. "Zimbabwe" is a popular corruption of the word "Zimbabgi" (Zimba or dzimba = houses; ibgi = stone), which the Makaranga apply to all or any of the numerous stone ruins to be found in Rhodesia. The "Zimbaoe," or chieftain's kraal, was never of stone, but built of poles and grass. "Zimba" or "Zimbaoe" (-oe is sometimes added as a locative suffix) is the nearest Makaranga equivalent to our English word 'home," referring to any set of buildings,— villages, cattle-kraals, granaries, and also the graves which are often to be found in rock fissures, blocked up with stones. The latter derivation might be criticised:[1] but it remains

[1] Thus, "zimba" (dzimba) and "zimbaoe" are not both plural words. "Dzimba," indeed, is the plural form of "imba" (=house). But "zimbaoe" (or better, "dzimbawe") is a singular form, having as plural "madzimbawe." The two words, then, could scarcely be synonymous.

clear that the words "Zimbabwe" and "Zimbaoe" (better, "dzimbawe") are applied by the Mashona natives to totally different objects. It is the confusion of these two words which has led some writers to identify the prehistoric, massive ruins at the Great Zimbabwe with the chief kraal or kraals of the Monomotapa.

Though the *Records* refer only to two kraals of the Monomotapa, yet we cannot suppose that the Monomotapa resided permanently in any particular spot. The native methods of agriculture soon exhaust the arable soil, and necessitate removal after a very few years. Add to this the superstition which requires the abandonment of a kraal upon the death of the chief, or in the event of any particular hut being struck by lightning. Furthermore, the insanitary conditions of a kraal are sufficient to render the spot uninhabitable after eight or ten years at most. Hence the royal kraals must have been constantly burnt down and re-built elsewhere, though it is probable that the Monomotapa never moved away altogether from the district, whether of Fura, or of Beza-Chidima. The facts show that in 1560-61, the Monomotapa's kraal was situated "close by" the river Musengezi, probably at N'pande.

In the light of Mr. R. N. Hall's minute knowledge of the early Portuguese records of South-Eastern Africa, it were well to correct a statement which appears now to be inaccurate. It has been said above, in connection with the empire of the Monomotapa, that "about half a century after Fr. Gonçalo's death, this phantom empire broke up into three or four principal states, . . ." (see chap. iv. *ad init.*) This opinion is held by many writers (cf. *World's History* (Heineman, 1903), vol. iii. p. 435); but it seems more probable that the disruption of the "empire" occurred some generations at least before the advent of Fr. da Silveira. Even in 1506 there was a tradition amongst the natives that the empire of the Monomotapa *formerly* included the kingdoms of Manica, Quiteve, and Sabia. (cf. Hall, *op. cit.* p. 393.) The predominance of the Makaranga over such a comparatively immense area is considered by Bantu authorities to be a resultant phase of the intercourse, in prehistoric times, with Arab, Persian, and Indian traders and miners. The mental and industrial superiority consequent to such intercourse and fusion led to the formation of the Makaranga "empire." As this foreign influence declined, the Makaranga gradually reverted to the true Bantu type, yet retaining many Semitic features of physique, language, and religion. This deterioration of an essentially unwarlike people was accompanied by a gradual dismemberment of the "empire" of the Monomotapa—a dismemberment which had already commenced when the Portuguese first arrived at Sofala in 1505. "It may be assumed, however," writes Mr. Hall (*op. cit.* p. 394), "that the 'empire,' even after its disruption, was the most powerful and most extensive Bantu domination yet known to research."

ROEHAMPTON:
PRINTED BY JOHN GRIFFI

www.ingramcontent.com/pod-product-compliance
Lightning Source LLC
Chambersburg PA
CBHW020426010526
44118CB00010B/443